# Classic
# INDIAN
# C·U·I·S·I·N·E

*Edited by Rosemary Moon*

**TIGER BOOKS INTERNATIONAL**
**LONDON**

ILLUSTRATIONS BY
CAMILLA SOPWITH AND SALLY BREWER

CLB 4366
This edition published 1995 by
Tiger Books International PLC, Twickenham
© 1995 CLB Publishing, Godalming, Surrey
Typeset by SX Composing, Rayleigh, Essex
All rights reserved
Printed and bound in South Africa
ISBN 1-85501-619-2

# CONTENTS

# INTRODUCTION

Indian cuisine justifiably ranks amongst the finest in the world. It is a fascinating amalgamation of the practices of many different cultures and religions, the best of each having been absorbed into the classic dishes of this great sub-continent.

## Indian Cooking in the West

There is no doubt at all that there is more interest in the west in Indian cookery than in any other style of ethnic food. In 1947 there was a maximum of six Indian restaurants in the UK – there are now around eight thousand and by 1987 there were more Indian restaurants than Chinese. Such is the interest in Indian food that it is now one of the most popular alternative styles of home cooking, not just for young people but for those of all ages. It is especially popular – and please do forgive this slightly sexist remark – with men who are weekend hobby-cooks and really enjoy a day dabbling in the kitchen. I often get asked to give fund-raising demonstrations for local schools and, without exception, those on Indian cookery are the best attended, with both mums and dads coming along and wanting the recipe sheets.

Whilst Thai and Mexican restaurants are only slowly becoming established in Europe, Chinese and Indian restaurants appear in almost every high street. It is interesting to note that Chinese food has adapted quite dramatically to suit the tastes of westerners, whereas Indian food has arrived making far fewer concessions to our preconceived ideas relating to food and culinary traditions. Probably the biggest change that has been required is the inclusion of starters on the typical Indian restaurant menu – such a concept of courses within a meal is virtually unknown to the majority of Indians. The more cosmopolitan communities in India have now adopted this western style of eating, previously only followed for banquets and celebratory meals.

The one slightly misleading impression that a western restaurant may give of classic Indian cookery is that it often features mushrooms. They are actually a fairly uncommon vegetable in India and are grown mainly in the far north, so the mushroom is not really a classic Indian ingredient.

## Sensible Shopping

With the explosion of interest in Indian cookery there have been many new products introduced in our shops in the way of sauces, pickles, chutneys and spice blends for various styles of cookery. My advice when selecting such items is to pick those made by an Indian company, rather than a multi-national. The flavours and textures will be far more authentic and there are likely to be fewer additional cereal thickening agents – many classic Indian dishes are actually thickened by the use of puréed vegetables such as onions, giving a more intense and brighter flavour to the dish than would be achieved with cornflour or any other cereal thickener.

I, in common with many other keen curry cooks, will travel miles out of my way to find my favourite curry pastes, pickles and chutneys. They are such a basic, integral part of successful Indian cooking that the store-cupboard can never contain too large a selection.

## The World's Great Religions

There are communities in India that follow just about all the great religions of the world, and each contributes to the classic cuisine of the country, through its customs and beliefs. Whilst many religions flourish in India there are two that dominate the country now, as they have throughout history. The followers of these religions are the Hindus and the Moslems.

## The Sacred Cow

The majority of Indians are Hindus and they do not eat beef or veal, as they regard the cow as sacred. This reverence is said to extend back to the start of civilisation as we know it, right back to the earliest farmers who decided that the nomadic life was not for them and that they would settle in one place. These first settlements were in the great river valleys of the Middle East and soon, as people began to want a patch of their own, the settlements spread as far as the Danube, across into China and down through Iran into India.

The early settlers grew crops and grazed cattle, one of the first animals to be domesticated. The cattle were kept for milk, meat and for leather. However, an expanding population meant that the cattle were soon in short supply and they were eventually kept more for their milk than for their meat. Once the Hindu religion was established the cow was regarded as sacred and was no longer eaten – this must have been one of the very earliest examples of a successful conservation project.

## The Moslem Influence

The Moguls, a Moslem people, invaded India from Central Asia in the sixteenth century, bringing with them many culinary customs including the halal kill, a method of slaughtering meat, and the tradition of never eating pork which is regarded as unclean. Considering that these people came from central Asia it is difficult to understand the ban on pork as it is so widely eaten throughout the continent and features strongly in the cuisine of many of India's neighbouring countries. However, the Moslems do not eat pork and so their meat cookery is based on sheep, goats and chicken.

It seems to me that the Moslem people are particularly good cooks. Their influence is strongest in northern India, where meat cookery is as its best and the food tends to be richer, cooked in plenty of ghee or butter.

## The Pork Dishes of the Goan Christians

There is pork in India – the Christian communities established in the times of the Portuguese settlers on the west coast around Goa have developed some classic pork curries containing coconut, mangoes and other local produce. This is really the only part of India where pig farming is carried out as, foragers that they are, pigs are not suited to life in dessert conditions.

When the British were established in India in the days of the Raj there was a fair exchange of ideas about cooking. One of the most famous dishes to emerge from around this time is kedgeree, said to have been made by the Scottish community in India who were pining for their beloved smoked haddock. Kedgeree is a mixture of smoked haddock, rice, hard-boiled eggs, onions and curry paste or spices. The curry paste is omitted by many people in the west but, to me, the dish is incomplete without it. Kedgeree is more usually served as a lunch or supper dish but it is also delicious at breakfast time – although I can understand leaving the spices out at that time of day!

## Afternoon Tea

During the days of the Raj another English custom became well-established amongst parts of the Indian community – that of afternoon tea and freshly cut sandwiches. This may sound rather bizarre amongst the traditional perception of classic Indian cookery, and there are no sandwich recipes contained in this book although banana sandwiches, perhaps developed in India, are one of my favourites! I have read an article by an established Indian cookery writer who is most grateful to the English for the introduction of the white loaf – a food that I would regard as a mixed blessing. Afternoon tea is very popular in India to this day amongst the professional people in larger cities.

## Parsee Traditions from Persia

One of my favourite styles of Indian cooking is that of the Parsees, a tribe who came to India from Persia and settled in Bombay and the neighbouring area of Gujarat. I find their food to be rich and complex in flavour, with subtle but imaginative use of fruits such as apricots. A typical Parsee garnish for meat dishes is deep-fried potato straws which provide a crisp

11

contrast to the curries with which they are served.

## Convenience Foods and Restaurants

When India gained its Independence in 1947 life began to change, especially in the cities and towns. Industrial and economic expansion meant that more women worked and there was less time to prepare many of the spices and chutneys that had traditionally been made in the home. Ghee, a clarified butter, had always been made at home and even the wheat for chapatis was ground into fine flour in each household using a chakki, two heavy millstones on top of each other.

The middle classes had always had domestic help and so many of the more tedious kitchen tasks would have been carried out by the staff. To a great extent this is now a way of life belonging to the past – more people live in flats without servants and there is simply not the room for the equipment required to carry on as before, or the time to undertake so much home processing of basic ingredients. So prepared chutneys, cooking fats and flour are now more widely available and commonly used than ever before but the basic skills of the Indian cook remain superb.

## Home Cooking is Best

Despite the proliferation of Indian restaurants in Europe it is interesting to note that very few families go to restaurants in India even now. It is a land of home cooking, where pride is taken in the preparation of food for friends and family and where the restaurants would have great difficulty in competing with the skills of even the average home cook. It is a privilege to be invited to an Indian home for a meal, an experience to be savoured. I have never had that pleasure but my father, who has visited India several times, has enjoyed a meal with colleagues in their home and talks about it at length! Nothing is too much trouble for an Indian family when they are entertaining – they have such a marvellous culinary tradition to share with you, bound up in a more than generous hospitality, and they go out of their way to make every mouthful as enjoyable as possible.

## Eating an Indian Meal

There are many customs that are changing in India and, in such a large country where there are the very rich and the exceptionally poor, it is difficult to say how a meal is most frequently served. Doubtless the middle classes and the vast majority of people living in the comfortable suburbs now eat using cutlery and china plates. However, this is something new and the traditional way of eating, still followed by the vast majority, is with the fingers and from a banana leaf which acts as a plate.

Meals are most commonly eaten in the kitchen – dining rooms are a very unusual feature in an Indian home. There is a ritual of hand and feet washing before a meal is begun and shoes are never worn in the kitchen. The food is very often prepared by the cook as he or she sits on the floor and the floor must therefore be kept as clean as possible, thus shoes are banned. However, time brings changes and some families now eat at a table in the kitchen and occasionally use a spoon to gather up any remaining food from their banana leaves or plates. The vast majority of Indians do still eat with their fingers, which is why breads are such an important feature in an Indian meal, being used as scoops for the food.

It is second nature for an Indian to wash his hands after a meal as well as before, to remove any stickiness from the food which has been eaten with the fingers. It is said that the tradition of rinsing the mouth after eating is responsible for the lack of dental treatment required by the average Indian during his lifetime.

## A Tradition of Home Baking

I meet so many people who say that they would like to make their own bread but that they simply do not have the time to do so. Well, that may be the case in England where bread is either raised with yeast or naturally fermented from a sourdough, but in India most breads are made at home and are quick both to prepare and to cook. This is because the vast majority of them are unleavened, and are simply mixed and then baked.

The easiest and quickest Indian bread must be the chapati. These are mixed, left for thirty minutes and then rolled out and cooked on a griddle or in a dry frying pan for about four minutes. The first time that we made them, my husband (who is really the bread maker in our house) was convinced that they were going to taste of cardboard but they were delicious! Do follow the recipe in this book and make a little foil packet to keep the finished chapatis warm whilst the others are cooking. It really is simple!

Breads were traditionally made by the ladies of the household and, as they are at their best when freshly cooked immediately before a meal, it became quite natural for the women to eat after everyone else, once they had finished the cooking.

When making a leavened Indian bread it is very easy for us to cover the dough and place it in an airing cupboard or similar warm place to rise, but the average Indian would not have an airing cupboard. Their traditional way of speeding the proving of the dough would be to warm a metal bowl with hot water, drain it and dry it and then to place the dough in the warmed bowl to rise – it is a simple method that works well.

The very finely ground flours that are used for making Indian breads are available in the west in healthfood shops and Indian grocers. It is difficult to get really good results without the correct flour but I have made reasonable chapatis using fine wholemeal pastry flour – traditional western wholemeal bread-making flour is far too coarse to give good results. It is interesting to note that although many of the Indian breads that are now sold in western supermarkets are made with white flour, the traditional Indian bread flour is wholemeal, although it is so finely ground that it is very pale in colour.

## A Rice Toddy

There is a most unusual bread that is made in the south of India – there is no recipe for it in this book as it would be difficult to source the ingredients but the description of it is most interesting. It is made with a rice flour, finely ground for bread making, and is leavened with toddy, not a restorative alcoholic drink but the fermented juice of the coconut palm.

## Rice – a Staple Food Synonymous with Curry

Although the phrase *curry and rice* trips off the tongue so readily that it could almost be said that one cannot exist without the other, this simply is not true. Some Indians are great rice eaters and it is their staple food, but there are many others who eat mainly bread and seldom have rice. It all depends on where they live. Roughly speaking, wheat is more widely grown in the north and west of India and these are the areas where bread is the staple food of the majority of people. Rice is grown throughout the south and in the central and northern river valleys. The city of Patna on the River Ganges in the north east of India is synonymous with rice the world over.

Around half of the world's population eat rice as their staple food and India is the second largest grower, producing nineteen per cent of the world's total crop. Rice needs moist, temperate conditions in which to grow and the rice fields, usually known as paddy fields, may be artificially flooded to provide the right conditions if they are not naturally moist enough. There are a few varieties of upland rice which grow well in drier conditions but these are not so common. The sowing and harvesting of rice has traditionally been done by hand, by workers standing in the flooded fields to sow the seeds or to plant out the seedlings. They later wade through the ripe crop, picking the husks of rice which resemble mature oats when ready for harvest. Seed is now sometimes sown from low-flying aircraft.

## To Process or not to Process

Grains of rice come well packaged! They are contained within an outer layer of husk which, when removed, reveals the protective bran. The rice at this stage is what we call brown rice and many people like to eat the rice with the bran which provides extra roughage in the diet. Care should be taken when cooking brown rice – never add salt to the water or use a salted stock as this will toughen the bran and the grain, retarding cooking and making it somewhat akin to a miniature bullet! The vast majority of rice is polished before it is packaged for the market, the polishing removing the bran and producing the white grains with which we are all familiar.

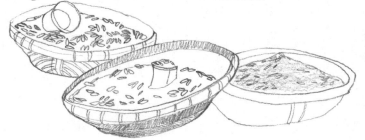

## Basmati Rice – the Best

Basmati rice is actually native to Pakistan, which borders the north west of India, but the fine, long-grain rice with a delicate flavour is the most popular for Indian cooking. The slogan to be found on so many Basmati rice packets proclaims that the grains are washed by the waters of the Himalayas – this certainly produces excellent rice.

## Wash it Well

Many rices are pre-washed in the west and, although such treatment ensures that they cook well with separate grains, it does reduce the flavour of the rice because of the extra processing. I prefer to buy white rice, preferably Basmati, and to wash it myself, removing all the excess starch from the grains and thus ensuring a good cooked result.

Other tips for cooking rice are given in the introduction to the rice recipes. However, one of my favourite ways of preparing it is not featured in this book so I will describe it here briefly. It is a method for cooking rice in the oven and is especially good when entertaining as it can just be left to its own devices.

This method is often used in Indian restaurants as the rice may be prepared and left for an hour or more without coming to any harm. You need a very large flameproof casserole, suitable for use on the hob and in the oven, that will allow the rice to boil without boiling over. It should have a tight-fitting lid but I have found that the rice cooks best if a stainless steel or enamelled casserole is used. Cast iron would seem to be a natural choice but, in my experience, it retains the heat so well that the rice tends to stick and dry out around the sides of the casserole. A good tip if using cast iron is to leave the rice in the oven for no longer than one hour.

Always use Basmati rice and wash it well. Use 275g/10oz rice to 570ml/1 pint liquid for the actual cooking of the rice. The rice should be weighed dry and then left to soak in water for at least 30 minutes. Drain the soaked rice in a sieve and discard the water. Bring the measured liquid to the boil in a separate pan – use water or a mixture of milk and water for a more flavoursome rice. Heat 1 tablespoon of ghee or unsalted butter in the flameproof casserole and fry a selection of spices, including bayleaves and a cinnamon stick, for 30 seconds, then add the rice and fry it until it is coated with the ghee and hot. Stir in the boiled liquid and return it quickly to the boil, cover and leave well alone over a medium to high heat for 8 minutes, ensuring that the rice does not boil over.

Look at the rice after 8 minutes – the liquid should have disappeared from the top of the pan, leaving the surface of the rice fully exposed. If this is not so, cover the pan again and cook for a further minute or two. Stir the rice briefly to ensure that it has not stuck to the bottom of the pan, then cover the casserole again and place it in the oven on its lowest setting. Leave it alone for at least one hour and you will have perfect rice. The timing of the boil, ensuring that all the liquid is gone from the surface of the rice before it is transferred to the oven, is the secret of success with this method of rice cookery.

## The Art of the Masala

Masala is a word that keeps cropping up in Indian culinary terminology. It is often used to describe a curry of medium heat but is actually defined as a combination of spices, or spices and herbs. A masala is therefore an essential part of almost every Indian dish (with the exception of some sweet ones) and it might be mild or so strong that it will make your eyes water! The blending of masalas indicates the skill of the cook. Garam masala is a mix of curry spices used as a basis for many dishes – it lacks much of the floury taste of some curry powders (a virtually unknown ingredient in India) and may be used as a garnish, added to a dish at the last moment. This is a store-cupboard essential for the keen curry cook.

## The Skill of Spicing

Westerners, and especially the British, have a reputation for under-seasoning their food, preferring it to be bland and somewhat dull. Well, if you are keen on Indian food that obviously is not an accurate description of your tastes! However, in order to achieve a good variety of flavours in your masalas and to really enjoy cooking authentic Indian food it is essential to have a good selection of spices in your store cupboard and to experiment with them to discover their flavours.

## Buying for Freshness

Once spices have been ground they start to deteriorate, so it is preferable to either grind them as you need them, or to buy them ready ground in small quantities which you use up quickly whilst the flavours are at their best. I would say that three months is the optimum storage time for ground spices, and that after six months they will be well on the way to staleness. Spice racks look very pretty on the kitchen wall but they do the spices stored in them no good at all. They are best kept in air-tight containers in a dark cupboard or drawer. I store most of mine in special containers with divided tops, allowing the spices to be shaken out or measured by the teaspoon, but I still keep the pots in a drawer.

Buying spices in small quantities will not necessarily ensure that they are fresh if you buy them from a small shop. I would therefore suggest that you buy date-stamped bottles or jars, an expensive way of purchasing but you will at least have a guide as to when the spices should be at their best. A cheaper way of buying, and the best way for a keen cook, is through a mail order company who will have a rapid turn-over of stock. I buy mine from a company in Stratford on Avon and never cease to be delighted with the freshness and fragrance of the goods.

## The Essential Indian Spices

Listing all the spices used in Indian cooking would take up pages of this book so I have picked a selection of the most commonly used, which are essential store-cupboard stock.

**Cardamoms** – there are two varieties, green and brown. The green are the most commonly used and are much smaller. The pods may be used whole, in which case they are often slightly opened at one end to allow the flavour of the seeds to escape. The seeds of the green cardamom may be used without the husks and should be lightly crushed before being added to either sweet or savoury dishes. Cardamoms are often used to flavour puddings – Cardamom & Honey Ice Cream (not a classic Indian recipe) is one of my favourite desserts.

**Cassia and Cinnamon** – these are actually two different spices but they are almost interchangeable, although cassia has a slightly less refined flavour and is therefore more suitable for savoury dishes than sweet. Cassia is sometimes called Chinese Cinnamon – both are used in Indian cookery.

**Chilli Powder** – adds most of the heat to a dry spice mix. It should be used judiciously until you are an experienced curry cook!

**Coriander** – this is easy to grow in the garden and grows well on the poorest of ground. It is used in three forms: the leaves are a fragrant garnish, and the seeds may be used whole (crushed and pressed into a leg of lamb before roasting they are quite delicious) or ground. The ground spice is mild and is frequently used by the tablespoonful rather than the teaspoon.

**Cumin** – ground cumin is the basis of so many masalas and is immediately identifiable by its fragrance. It is slightly sharp. Cumin seeds are usually roasted to release their flavour before being used.

**Mustard Seeds** – there are three types: black, brown and white, but it is the latter that is most commonly used in Indian cookery. Mustard seeds are used whole or lightly crushed to release their flavour. They make a particularly successful marinade for shellfish such as prawns.

**Poppy Seeds** – are not really a spice but they are a valuable flavouring. They may be blue or white and add a distinctive nutty flavour and texture to many dishes. Some recipes call for them to be crushed but I prefer to leave them whole – they are delightful in kormas and other creamy curries.

**Turmeric** – This is a ground, dried tuber, used for its mild flavour and for its striking yellow colour. Often nick-named 'poor man's saffron', it should not be used as a colouring in dishes where its distinctive flavour will dominate other ingredients.

**Creamed Coconut** is not a spice but it is another invaluable store-cupboard ingredient for the keen curry cook. It is sold in a block and is a rich, creamy coconut preparation which should be crumbled before being added to a hot masala or sauce, and then stirred until dissolved. It has a much better flavour and texture than desiccated coconut and is not only more affordable but easier to use than canned coconut milk.

### Frying over a Low Heat

There are two golden rules for cooking with ground spices. The first is that they must always be cooked in a little hot fat, usually with onions or other vegetables that require pre-cooking, to remove any floury, uncooked flavour. The second rule is that this cooking should take place over a very low heat, to ensure that the spices do not burn. Many of the recipes given in this book go to great lengths to explain the heat that should be used for various processes. It is essential that the instructions given are carefully followed to ensure that the best results and flavours are obtained from all the ingredients in any dish. Burnt spices contribute nothing except a bitter aftertaste to a dish.

## Salt and Pepper

These essential seasonings are of paramount importance in any cuisine. Salt is especially important in Indian cookery as it brings out the flavours of otherwise bland dishes. I remember in my very early days of demonstrating that I had invited a class to taste a red lentil daal and that there had been very little comment about it. Convinced that it would be as delicious as usual I took a large spoonful as soon as everyone had left and realised immediately that it hadn't even seen the salt pot – it was ghastly! Many recipes actually specify the amount of salt to be added to a dish although it may of course be adjusted to suit your individual taste at the end of the cooking period. As spoon measures in recipes are always taken as level measures you will find that some recipes call for one and a quarter teaspoons of salt – this may easily be converted to one heaped teaspoon.

Before chillies arrived in India in the late fifteenth century – they were native to Mexico and were quickly introduced to other parts of the world by Spanish and Portuguese explorers – most Indian recipes relied on peppercorns for their heat. Indian, or Tellicherry, peppercorns are small and very hot. They are my favourite peppercorns (I buy them by mail order from Stratford on Avon) but they need to be finely ground or unsuspecting guests may be surprised by their fire.

## Tea – One of India's Greatest Exports

Well, that's my opinion but then I'm a tea addict! India and China are the two greatest quality tea producing nations but India produces more 'normal' teas – many China teas are lightly smoked or fermented for extra flavour.

Assam, the region that appears to have been tacked onto the north-east of India, produces fine strong teas that are popular throughout the world. Assam is an ideal tea for early morning with its robust flavour and rich brown colour. Darjeeling, the champagne tea, is the other great Indian variety. It is grown in the foothills of the Himalayas and has a light, delicate scent and flavour. It is the perfect afternoon tea and is often drunk black. Earl Grey, another of the most popular teas, is actually a blend of Indian and China black teas which is flavoured with oil of bergamot. A true Earl Grey blend has to be made with both Indian and China teas – for many years inferior blends were sold containing bergamot and one or other of the black teas but not both.

The classic cuisine of India has so much to offer. There is much more to it than two or three varieties of curry and it may take many years to learn all the secrets of gourmet Indian cookery. Do remember that mild and creamy dishes have just as much to offer as burningly hot ones, and that they will suit the majority of your friends and family much better than the 'total experience' dishes! I hope that the selection of classic recipes in this book will be as much of an inspiration to you as it has been to me.

# STARTERS & SNACKS

For the vast majority of Indians the concept of a meal made up of various courses is virtually unknown. It is an idea that has been adopted by the owners of numerous Indian restaurants to appease our western perceptions of how a meal should be served.

Snacks are, however, very popular and whilst many are bought ready-made in the countless street markets in every town, there are some that are best cooked at home. Onion bhajis certainly fall into this category as they need to be piping hot, and served immediately after cooking, to be at their best.

## Soup – a Thin Curry

There are surprisingly few soups within the classic Indian cuisine. Perhaps this is because the idea of a starter only exists in the homes of the better-off city dwellers, but I feel that the more likely explanation is that a simple dish of dhal is more filling and nutritious than a soup would be. However, those who do eat soup often refer to it as a thin curry, and to a masala as a thick curry.

## Samosas, the Perfect Snack

Meat and vegetable samosas have become two of the most popular foods in the delicatessen counters of the modern western supermarket. They are deep-fried parcels enclosing a spicy filling which are really superb when eaten hot. Samosas are usually triangular in shape and I find the folding and shaping of the pastry to be an art in itself! Unfortunately, the fact that so many supermarkets now sell samosas means that many people eat them cold, when they are quite definitely not at their best, and they never experience the true glory of these delicious snacks.

The first time that I tried a home-made samosa was at a party at the BBC's Pebble Mill studios in Birmingham. They were made by a researcher on the Pebble Mill programme and were an absolute revelation. I resolved then and there never to buy ready-made samosas again and I never have. I must, however, admit to a certain amount of cheating. There is a recipe for samosa pastry in this book, but you may prefer to use some of the excellent filo pastry that is now available in most supermarkets. Brush the sheets with melted ghee or butter and proceed with the folding and shaping as directed in the recipe. Always allow the stuffing mixture to cool completely before filling the samosas otherwise the inside of the pastry may sweat and become soggy.

## Chicken Tikka – a Popular Restaurant Starter

Chicken Tikka is traditionally cooked in a clay oven, a tandoor, and is one of the classic dishes from the Punjab region of northern India. Cubes of marinated, spiced chicken are threaded onto skewers and baked quickly, producing a succulent dry spiced dish. I would serve Chicken Tikka with a raita, a tomato or onion salad and puris or other small Indian breads. This recipe provides the base for the extremely popular Chicken Tikka Masala, but do remember to prepare the tikka before embarking on the masala sauce.

### Pakoras – Deep-fried Fritters

Another dish originally from the Punjab but which is now popular throughout India is the pakora, a deep-fried fritter, traditionally made with vegetables but left-over cooked chicken is now sometimes used. There is a crisp-like snack available in the west called a pakora but it bears little resemblance to those that I have tasted in good restaurants.

The basic pakora batter is spiced and often contains some whole spices as well as ground. Almost any vegetable can be prepared as a pakora – cauliflower and potato are my favourites – but the secret of success is to ensure that the pieces of vegetable are completely covered with the batter before they are fried. This prevents the vegetables from becoming greasy and ensures an even, crisp cook.

### Onion Bhajis – a Favourite Dish

The first time that I made onion bhajis they were an unqualified disaster, simply because I like them so much that I thought I would make big ones – a big mistake! The bhajis are sliced or shredded onions coated in a thick batter and then fried, quite a simple cooking process but one that I totally messed up by making my bhajis too big. As I now know only too well, if they are too large the bhajhis will not cook in the middle before they are cooked on the outside, so the golden rule is to keep them only a little larger than bite-sized. I can assure you that, in this case, small is best!

# DHAL SOUP

*This is a thick warming lentil soup, lightly spiced and suitable for hot and cold days alike.*

Serves 6

### INGREDIENTS

340g/12oz red or yellow lentils
850ml/1½ pints water or stock
4 canned tomatoes, drained and crushed
1 green chilli, sliced lengthways and seeded
2 tbsps natural yogurt or soured cream
15g/½oz butter
1 onion, chopped, or sliced into rings
Salt and freshly ground black pepper
Freshly chopped coriander leaves to garnish

Wash the lentils in 4-5 changes of water. Drain them well and put them into a large pan with the water or stock. Cover the pan and bring the lentils to the boil over a moderate heat. Reduce the heat and simmer for about 10-15 minutes, or until the lentils are soft. You may need to add extra water. Using a balloon whisk, beat the lentils until they are smooth. Add the tomatoes and chilli and simmer for 2 minutes, then stir in the yogurt or soured cream. Reheat, but do not boil.

Melt the butter in a small pan and fry the onion gently, until it is soft, but not coloured.

Pour the soup into serving bowls and scatter with the chopped coriander and fried onion. Discard the green chillies before eating the soup.

# ONION BHAJIS

*These Onion Bhajis are one of the most popular starters in Western Indian restaurants, as well as being firm favourites all over India. They are shredded onions coated in a lightly spiced batter which is then deep-fried.*

Serves 6-8

### INGREDIENTS

175g/6oz besan (gram or chick-pea flour)
1 tsp salt
Pinch of bicarbonate of soda
1 tbsp ground rice
2 tsps ground cumin
2 tsps ground coriander
½-1 tsp chilli powder
1-2 fresh green chillies, finely chopped and seeded if a milder flavour is preferred
2 large onions, sliced into half rings and separated
200ml/7 fl oz water
Oil for deep-frying

Sieve the besan and add the salt, bicarbonate of soda, ground rice, cumin, coriander, chilli powder and green chillies; mix well. Add the onions and mix thoroughly, then gradually add the water and keep mixing until a soft but thick batter is formed and the onions are thoroughly coated with the batter.

Heat the oil over medium heat (*it is important to heat the oil to the correct temperature: 160-180°C*). To test the temperature, take a tiny amount of the batter, and drop it in the oil. If it floats up to the surface immediately but without turning brown, the oil is at the correct temperature. Using a tablespoon, add as many half spoonfuls of the onion mix as the pan will hold in a single layer. Take care not to make them too large as this will result in the outside of the bhajis being overdone while the insides remain uncooked, a common problem. Reduce the heat to low as the bhajis need to be fried over a gentle heat to ensure that the batter at the centre of the bhajis is cooked, and stays soft, whilst the outside turns golden brown and crisp. This should take about 10-12 minutes for each batch. Drain the bhajis on absorbent kitchen paper, before serving.

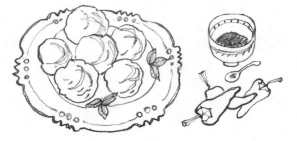

# CHICKEN OR TURKEY PAKORAS

*I have suggested fresh meat for the recipe below, but you could easily make these pakoras with left-over poultry from a roast.*

Serves 6-8

### INGREDIENTS
150ml/¼ pint water
1 onion, roughly chopped
2-3 cloves garlic, peeled and roughly chopped
1-2 fresh green chillies, roughly chopped; remove the seeds if you prefer a mild flavour
2 tbsps freshly chopped coriander leaves
150g/5oz besan (gram flour or chick pea flour), sieved
1 tsp ground coriander
1 tsp ground cumin
½ tsp garam masala
½ tsp chilli powder
1 tsp salt
Pinch of bicarbonate of soda
340g/12oz fresh, boneless and skinless chicken or turkey breast
Oil for deep-frying

Put 90ml/3 fl oz water from the measured amount into a liquidiser with the onion, garlic, green chillies and coriander leaves, and blend until smooth.

Alternatively, process the ingredients in a food processor without the water. Mix the besan, coriander, cumin, garam masala, chilli powder, salt and bicarbonate of soda together in a large bowl. Add the liquidised ingredients and mix thoroughly, then add the remaining water and mix well to form a thick paste. Cut the chicken into pieces and add them to the paste, turning until the chicken is well coated.

Heat the oil over a medium heat; when hot, add one piece of besan-coated chicken at a time from a tablespoon until there are as many pieces as the pan will hold in a single layer without overcrowding. Make certain that each piece is fully coated with the paste before adding it to the pan. Reduce the heat and fry the pakoras for 10-15 minutes, turning them over half way through cooking. Remove the pakoras with a slotted spoon and drain on absorbent kitchen paper.

# BOTI KABAB

*Lamb is my favourite meat for curries and other Indian foods. Serve these kebabs on their skewers as a starter or serve individual pieces of the lamb on cocktail sticks for drinks party nibbles.*

Serves 6

*INGREDIENTS*
680g/1½lbs boneless leg of lamb
2 small cloves of garlic, peeled and chopped
2 tbsps freshly chopped coriander leaves
2 tbsps lemon juice
6 tbsps thick-set natural yogurt
Salt
½ tsp ground turmeric
2 tbsps cooking oil

6 green cardamoms (with the skin)
1 cinnamon stick, 1 inch long
2-3 dried red chillies
1 tbsp coriander seeds

*To Garnish*
Thinly sliced onions rings, separated
Crisp lettuce leaves
Wedges of cucumber

Prick the meat all over with a sharp knife and cut into 4cm/1½-inch cubes. Place the garlic, coriander leaves, lemon juice and yogurt in a liquidiser or food processor and blend until smooth. Add the salt and turmeric. Grind the remaining spices together and add to the yogurt. Put the meat into a bowl and add the liquidised ingredients. Mix thoroughly, cover, and leave to marinate for 6-8 hours (or overnight in the refrigerator).

Preheat the grill to high. Line the grill pan with a piece of aluminium foil (this will reflect heat and also keep your grill pan clean). Thread the meat onto skewers leaving about a 6mm/¼ inch gap between each piece. Mix any remaining marinade with the oil. Place the skewers on the prepared grill pan and grill the kababs for 2-3 minutes, then turn and grill for a further 2-3 minutes. Reduce the heat to medium. Brush the kababs with the oil and marinade mixture and grill for a further 6-8 minutes. Turn the skewers over and baste again with the remaining marinade mixture. Grill for a further 6-8 mintues, then serve immediately.

# POTATO PAKORAS

*Potatoes are my favourite vegetable to make into pakoras – I like the smooth texture hidden inside the crispy, spiced batter.*

Serves 4-6

### INGREDIENTS
60g/2oz besan (gram flour or chick pea flour)
1 tbsp ground rice
½ tsp salt
1½ tsps ground coriander
1 tsp ground cumin
½ tsp chilli powder
60ml/2 fl oz water
460g/1lb potatoes, peeled and cut into 6mm/¼ inch thick slices
Oil for deep-frying

Mix all the dry ingredients together in a large bowl, then add the water and mix to thick paste. Add the potatoes and mix until the slices are completely coated with the paste.

Heat the oil over a medium heat in a deep pan (you can use a deep fat fryer or a chip pan without the basket) to about 170°C. Add as many of the coated potato slices as the pan will hold in a single layer. Fry the pakoras until golden brown – about 6-8 minutes. Drain on absorbent kitchen paper before serving.

# MEAT SAMOSAS

*I find that meat samosas make an excellent light lunch or supper dish. The first time that I tasted homemade samosas I resolved never to buy ready-made ones again – they are delicious!*

Makes 18 samosas

### INGREDIENTS
2 tbsps cooking oil
2 onions, finely chopped
225g/8oz lean minced lamb or beef
3-4 cloves garlic, peeled and crushed
1.25cm/ ½-inch piece of fresh root ginger, finely grated
½ tsp ground turmeric
2 tsps ground coriander
1½ tsps ground cumin
½-1 tsp chilli powder
½ tsp salt
120ml/4 fl oz warm water
175g/6oz frozen peas
2 tbsps desiccated coconut
1 tsp garam masala
1-2 fresh green chillies, finely chopped and seeded if a milder flavour is preferred
2 tbsps freshly chopped coriander leaves
1 tbsp lemon juice

Heat the oil over a medium heat and fry the onions until they are lightly browned. Add the mince, garlic and ginger. Stir and fry until all the liquid evaporates then reduce the heat. Add the turmeric, coriander, cumin, chilli powder and salt. Stir and cook until the mince is lightly browned. Add the water and the peas, bring to the boil, cover and simmer for 25-30 minutes. If any liquid remains, cook uncovered for 4-5 minutes until the meat is completely dry, stirring frequently. Stir in the coconut, garam masala, green chillies and coriander leaves. Remove from the heat and add the lemon juice. Cool thoroughly before filling the samosas.

### For the Pastry
225g/8oz plain flour
60g/2oz ghee or butter
½ tsp salt
75ml/2½ fl oz warm water
Oil for deep-frying

Add the butter and salt to the flour and rub in well. Mix to a soft dough by adding the water. Knead until the dough feels soft and velvety to the touch. Divide the dough into 9 pieces. Roll into balls between the palms of your hands and then press down to make flat cakes. Roll out into 10cm/4 inch dics and cut each into two. Use each semicircle of pastry as one envelope.

Moisten the straight edge with a little warm water, then fold the semicircle of pastry in half to form a triangular cone. Join the straight edges by pressing them hard into each other. Make sure that there are no gaps. Add the filling, leaving a small border at the top of the cone, then moisten the top edges and press them hard together. Deep-fry the samosas over gentle heat until they are golden brown and drain on absorbent kitchen paper.

# SEEKH KABABS

*Seekh kababs were the first Indian kababs that I ever tried and I have been a fan ever since! They can be cooked on metal skewers, but the bamboo type are much more convenient.*

Makes 18 kababs

### INGREDIENTS
Juice of ½ lemon
2 tbsps freshly chopped fresh mint *or* 1 tsp dried or bottled mint
3-4 tbsps freshly chopped coriander leaves
30g/1oz raw cashews
1 onion, roughly chopped
2 small cloves of glaric, peeled and roughly chopped
1-2 fresh green chillies, finely chopped or minced; remove the seeds if you like it mild
680g/1½ lbs lean minced meat, beef or lamb
2 tsps ground coriander
2 tsps ground cumin
1 tsp ground ajwain (ajowan or carum) or ground caraway seeds
½ tsp garam masala
½ tsp tandoori colour *or* a few drops of red food colouring mixed with 1 tbsp tomato purée
½ tsp freshly ground black pepper
1 egg yolk
¼ tsp chilli powder
1 tsp salt
2 tbsps white poppy seeds, ground
2 tbsps sesame seeds, ground
4 tbsps cooking oil

Place the lemon juice, mint, coriander leaves, cashews, onion, garlic and green chillies in a liquidiser or food processor and blend to a smooth paste. Transfer the mixture to a large bowl. Using the liquidiser or processor, grind the mince in 2-3 small batches until it is fairly smooth, rather like a paste. Add the meat to the rest of the liquidised ingredients in the bowl. Add the remaining ingredients, except the oil, and knead the mixture thoroughly until it is smooth. Alternatively, put all the ingredients, except the oil, in an electric food processor and process until the mixture is smooth. Chill for 30 minutes.

Preheat oven to 240°C/475°F, Gas Mark 9. Line a roasting tin with aluminium foil. Divide the kebab mix into 18 pieces, form each piece into a sausage shape around a wooden skewer by rolling it between your hands. Place in the prepared roasting tin. Make the rest of the kababs the same way. Brush generously with the oil and place the roasting tin just below the top rung of the oven. Cook for 6-8 minutes. Remove the tin from the oven and brush the kababs liberally with the remaining oil and cook for a further 6-8 minutes.

Allow the kababs to cool slightly before removing them from the skewers, or serve them on the skewers.

# NARGISI KABABS

*These tasty meat balls with a surprise filling are more like patties than kababs. Use finely minced beef or lamb as coarser meat will split during cooking and allow the filling to escape.*

Makes 14 kababs

*INGREDIENTS*
*For the Filling*
2 hard-boiled eggs, shelled and roughly chopped
1 fresh green chilli, finely chopped; remove the seeds if you prefer a mild flavour
2 tbsps finely chopped or minced onion
1 tbsp finely chopped or minced coriander leaves
¼ tsp salt
1 tbsp thick-set natural yogurt

30g/1oz ghee or unsalted butter
1 large onion, coarsely chopped
3-4 cloves garlic, peeled and roughly chopped
2.5cm/1 inch piece of fresh root ginger, peeled and roughly chopped

1 tsp ground cumin
1½ tsps ground coriander
1 tsp garam masala
½ tsp chilli powder
½ tsp freshly ground black pepper
3 tbsps thick-set natural yogurt
1 tbsp fresh mint leaves *or* 1 tsp dried or bottle mint
2 tbsps freshly chopped coriander leaves
¾ tsp salt
570g/1¼lbs lean lamb or beef, finely minced
1 egg
2 tbsps besan (chick pea flour or gram flour), sieved
1 tbsp water
90ml/3 fl oz cooking oil

Combine all ingredients for the filling in a bowl, mix thoroughly and set to one side. Melt the ghee or butter over medium heat and fry the onion, garlic and ginger for 3-4 minutes. Reduce the heat and add the cumin, coriander, garam masala, chilli powder and pepper, stir fry for 1-2 minutes, then remove from the heat and allow to cool.

Place the yogurt in a liquidiser or food processor and add the fried ingredients, the mint, coriander, salt and the mince. Blend until smooth. If you are using a liquidiser, blend the ingredients first without the mince. Transfer the blended ingredients to a mixing bowl and process the mince in 2-3 batches. Knead the blended ingredients and the mince until smooth. Divide the mixture into portions. Make a depression in the centre of each ball and form into a cup shape. Fill with 1 heaped tsp of the egg mixture and cover the filling by pressing the edges together. Roll gently between the palms of your hands to form a neat ball, press the ball gently and form a round flat cake about 2cm/¾ inch thick. Make the rest of the kababs the same way.

Beat the egg and gradually add the besan while still beating. Add the water and beat again. Heat the oil in a wide, shallow pan, preferably non-stick or cast iron, over a medium heat. Dip each kabab in the egg batter and fry in a single layer without overcrowding the pan. Cook for 3-4 minutes on each side until browned. Drain on absorbent kitchen paper before serving.

# CAULIFLOWER PAKORAS

*A pakora is a spicy Indian snack, fried in a light batter until crispy. Serve plain as finger food, or with a salad garnish and chutneys as a starter.*

Serves 4

*INGREDIENTS*
90g/3oz besan (gram flour or
  chick pea flour), sieved
1 tbsp ground rice
¾ tsp salt
2 tbsps ground coriander
2 tsps ground cumin
½-1 tsp chilli powder
½ tsp ground turmeric
Pinch of bicarbonate of soda
1 cauliflower, cut into 4cm/1½
  inch florets
150ml/¼ pint water
Oil for deep-frying

Mix all the dry ingredients in a large bowl, then add the cauliflower and water. Mix until the cauliflower is fully coated with the batter.

Heat the oil over a medium heat to around 170°C and add as many florets as the pan will hold in a single layer. You can use a deep fat fryer or a chip pan without the basket. Fry until the pakoras are uniformly brown – this will take about 5 minutes. Drain on absorbent kitchen paper, and serve hot.

# SPICED MIXED NUTS

*Anyone addicted to dry roasted peanuts will adore these spiced nuts! They might keep in a screw-topped jar if given the chance!*

Serves 8-10

## INGREDIENTS
120g/4oz whole almonds
120g/4oz raw cashews
2 tsps cooking oil
½ tsp ground coriander
½ tsp ground cumin
¼ tsp chilli powder
½ tsp salt

Cook the nuts for 3-4 minutes in a heavy based frying pan over a low heat until the nuts are just heated through. Add 1 tsp oil, stir and mix thoroughly. Toast the nuts until they are evenly browned, stirring constantly. This may take up to 10 minutes. Remove from the heat and sprinkle with the spices and salt immediately. Mix thoroughly, then leave for 10 minutes. Add the remaining oil, stir and mix until the nuts are fully coated by the spcies.

Allow to cool completely before serving.

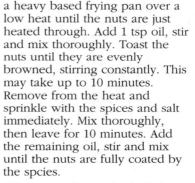

# SPICED POTATO BITES

*Potatoes are not just a vegetable to serve with meat in Indian cookery! They are used in many inventive ways, such as this cocktail nibble of spiced potatoes, to be served on sticks with drinks.*

Serves 6-8

INGREDIENTS
680g/1½lbs potatoes
4 tbsps cooking oil
½ tbsp salt
¼ tsp garam masala
½ tsp ground cumin
½ tsp ground coriander
¼-½ tsp chilli powder

Boil the potatoes in their jackets, cool then peel and dice into 2.5cm/1-inch cubes. Heat the oil over a medium heat in a wide shallow pan, preferably non-stick or cast iron. It is important to have the right pan otherwise the potatoes will stick. Add the potatoes and spread them evenly around the pan. Brown the potatoes evenly, stirring them occasionally. When the potatoes are brown, sprinkle them with the salt, garam masala, cumin, coriander and the chilli powder. Stir gently until the potatoes are fully coated with the spices. Remove from the heat, and serve on cocktail sticks or with a salad garnish.

# VEGETABLE SAMOSAS

*These popular parcels of spicy vegetables are now available in just about every supermarket and delicatessen. It really is worth making your own – they are so much better!*

Makes 18 samosas

## INGREDIENTS

460g/1lb potatoes
2 tbsps cooking oil
½ tsp black mustard seeds
1 tsp cumin seeds
2 dried red chillies, roughly chopped
1 onion, finely chopped
1-2 fresh green chillies, roughly chopped and seeded if a milder flavour is preferred
½ tsp ground turmeric
1 tsp ground coriander
1 tsp ground cumin
1 tsp salt
1 tbsp freshly chopped coriander leaves
Samosa pastry, see Meat Samosas

Boil the potatoes in their jackets, allow to cool then peel and dice them. Heat the oil and add the mustard seeds. As soon as they start crackling, add the cumin seeds and red chillies, and then the onions and green chillies. Fry until the onions are soft, then add the turmeric, coriander and cumin. Stir quickly and add the potatoes and the salt. Reduce the heat to low, and stir-fry until the potatoes are thoroughly mixed with the spices. Remove from the heat and stir in the coriander leaves. Cool thoroughly before filling the samosas. Make up the pastry and complete the Samosas following the method for Meat Samosas.

# BARRAH KABAB (MARINATED LAMB CHOPS)

*This delicious spiced lamb dish may be served as a starter or a main course. The yogurt tenderises the lamb before cooking.*

Serves 6-8

### INGREDIENTS

900g/2lbs lamb chump chops
½ tsp ground nutmeg
½ tsp ground black pepper
½ tsp ground cinnamon
½ tsp cayenne or chilli powder
½ tsp ground turmeric
2 cloves garlic, peeled
2 tbsps roughly chopped onions
1.25cm/½ inch piece of fresh root ginger, peeled and chopped
150ml/¼ pint thick-set natural yogurt
½ tsp salt
1 tbsp cooking oil
1 tsp ground cumin
1 tbsp sesame seeds

Trim off any excess fat from the chops and flatten each one with a meat mallet or a rolling pin. Place all ingredients except the chops, oil, cumin and sesame seeds, into a liquidiser or food processor and blend to a purée. Place the chops in a large bowl and pour the blended ingredients over them. Rub the marinade into each chop with your fingers, then cover and leave to marinate for at least 8 hours in a cool place or overnight in the refrigerator.

Preheat oven to 20°C/425°F/Gas Mark 7. Line a roasting tin with aluminium foil (this will help reflect heat and keep your roasting tin clean). Arrange the chops in the roasting tin in a single layer (reserve any remaining marinade) and cook in the centre of the oven for 10 minutes – turn the chops over once. Reduce the heat to 200°C/400°F/Gas Mark 6. Mix the remaining marinade with the oil and cumin. Brush the chops with this and sprinkle half the sesame seeds on top. Return the tray to the upper part of the oven for 10 minutes. Turn the chops over and brush with the remaining marinade mixture and add the rest of the sesame seeds as before. Cook for a further 10-15 minutes, until the meat is tender.

# MUTTON PATTIES

*These little mutton patties are now most commonly made
with lamb, although beef could be used if preferred. Serve
with a tomato and onion salad and chutneys.*

Makes 14 patties

### INGREDIENTS
1kg/2¼lbs potatoes
½-1 tsp chilli powder
1½ tsps salt
3 tbsps cooking oil
½ tsp fennel seeds
1 large onion, finely chopped
1.25cm/½ inch piece of fresh
   root ginger, peeled and finely
   grated
2-4 cloves garlic, peeled and
   chopped or crushed
340g/12oz fine lean minced lamb

1 tsp ground cumin
1½ tsps ground coriander
1 tsp ground fennel
½ tsp ground turmeric
½ tsp garam masala
3 tbsps water

200g/7oz can tomatoes
90ml/3 fl oz water
1 fresh green chilli, finely
   chopped
2 tbsps freshly chopped
   coriander leaves
1 egg, beaten
2 tbsps milk
2 tbsps flour
120g/4oz golden breadcrumbs
Oil for deep-frying

Boil the potatoes in their jackets, cool slightly then peel and mash them. Add half the chilli powder and ½ tsp salt from the measured amount. Divide the mixture into 14 portions, cover and set aside. Heat the oil over a medium heat and fry the fennel seeds until they are brown. Add the onions, ginger and garlic, and fry until the onions are lightly browned. Add the mince and fry until all moisture evaporates, stirring frequently – this may take 5 minutes or so. Mix the spices with the water and add the spice paste to the pan. Cook for 5-6 minutes, reducing the heat towards the last 2-3 minutes. Raise the heat and add the tomatoes, breaking them up with the back of the spoon. Cook for 3-4 minutes, stirring frequently, then add the water, the remaining chilli powder and salt, then cover and simmer for 15 minutes. Cook, uncovered, for a further 4-5 minutes or until the mixture is completely dry but moist. Stir frequently. Stir in the chopped green chilli and the coriander leaves. Cook for 1-2 minutes then remove from the heat and allow to cool completely.

Mix the beaten egg with the milk and set aside. Take a portion of the potato and roll it into a ball. Make a depression in the centre and form into a cup shape. Fill the cavity with a little mince leaving a border around the filling. Ease the potato around the meat to completely enclose the filling then flatten to form a round cake, about 1.25cm½ inch thick. Use the potato and minced meat to make 14 of the patties. Dust the patties in the flour then dip in egg and milk mixture and roll in the breadcrumbs. Deep fry the patties until they are golden brown, in about 6-8 minutes. Drain on absorbent kitchen paper.

# CHICKEN TIKKA

*Of all the Indian restaurant starters I think that this is the most popular! It should be cooked in a tandoor, an Indian clay oven, but this recipe is adapted for a standard gas or electric oven.*

Serves 4

*INGREDIENTS*
460g/1lb boneless chicken breast, skinned
1 tsp salt
Juice of ½ lemon
½ tsp tandoori colour *or* a few drops of red food colouring mixed with 1 tbsp tomato purée
2 cloves garlic, peeled and roughly chopped
1.25cm/½ inch piece of fresh root ginger, peeled and roughly chopped
2 tsps ground coriander
½ tsp ground allspice or garam masala
¼ of a whole nutmeg, finely grated
½ tsp ground turmeric
150ml/¼ pint thick-set natural yogurt
4 tbsps corn or vegetable oil
½ tsp chilli powder

Cut the chicken into 2.5cm/1 inch cubes. Sprinkle with ½ tsp salt from the measured amount, and the lemon juice – mix thoroughly, cover and leave for 30 minutes. Place the rest of the ingredients in a liquidiser or food processor and blend until smooth. Strain the sauce over the chicken through a sieve – force the mixture through using the back of a spoon and discard anything left in the sieve. Coat the chicken thoroughly with the sieved marinade, cover, and leave to marinate for 6-8 hours or overnight in the refrigerator.

Preheat the oven to 230°C/450°F/Gas Mark 8. Line a roasting tin with aluminium foil (this will help to maintain the high level of temperature required to cook the chicken quickly without drying it out). Thread the chicken pieces onto skewers, leaving a 6mm/¼-inch gap between each piece (this is necessary for the heat to reach all sides of the chicken). Place the skewers in the prepared roasting tin and brush with some of the remaining marinade. Cook in the centre of the oven for 6-8 minutes. Turn the skewers over and brush the pieces of chicken with the remaining marinade. Return the tin to the oven and cook for a further 6-8 minutes. Shake off any excess liquid from the chicken. (Strain the excess liquid and keep aside for Chicken Tikka Masala.) Place the skewers on a serving dish. You may take the tikka off the skewers if you wish, but allow the meat to cool slightly before removing it from the skewers.

# DHINGRI KARI
# (MUSHROOM CURRY)

*This mushroom curry is not too hot but does have a fairly robust flavour. I would serve it with brown rice as a starter.*

Serves 4

### INGREDIENTS

225g/8oz leeks, finely sliced
2 cloves garlic, peeled and
  crushed
½ tsp fresh root ginger, peeled
  and grated
2 tsps curry powder
1 tsp garam masala
2 tbsps oil
460g/1lb mushrooms, cut into
  quarters
120g/4oz creamed coconut,
  grated
1 tbsp lemon juice
Salt

Fry the leeks, garlic, ginger and spices in the oil until soft. Add the mushrooms and cook over a low heat until soft, then add the grated coconut and cook gently until the coconut has completely dissolved, adding a little water if the mixture appears too dry. Stir in the lemon juice and sufficient salt to taste. Serve on a bed of rice.

# FISH & SHELLFISH

I am certain that most people who have eaten in an Indian restaurant have tried a king prawn masala or a prawn biryani. I have no figures to support my theory but I am certain that prawns are second only to chicken as the most popular main ingredient in restaurant curries.

## The Ubiquitous Prawn

Excellent prawns are caught off the Indian coast and they are often exported as their quality is so good. The prawns range in size from what we would call shrimps to enormous king prawns, sometimes weighing up to half a kilo each. Such a range of sizes has allowed a vast number of prawn recipes to be developed over the years. The smaller prawns, the ones of a size more familiar to us, make the best curries in as much as they can easily be coated with a sauce, completely absorbing the flavours and becoming a deliciously integrated dish. Larger prawns may be scattered with spices and brushed with oil, then baked or grilled. Prawns are sometimes marinated in yogurt and spices (mustard seed works particularly well) but my favourite way of cooking them is with onion, garlic, green chillies and creamed coconut. I add a little pickle and tomato purée and, within 10 minutes, I have a dish that is utterly delicious.

Tasty as they are it is, however, a great pity that prawns are so totally dominant in the fish department of the average Indian restaurant. I can understand why – they are still considered to be a treat (hence the enduring popularity of the ubiquitous prawn cocktail) but there are plenty of other fish which I feel make better curries than these endlessly popular shellfish.

The best Indian fish dish that I have ever tasted was a baked mackerel, served as part of a Sunday lunch-time buffet at 'Chutney Mary's' in the Fulham Road. Mackerel are caught off the south east coast of India and their robust flavour and firm texture are the perfect medium for spicy, Indian cookery. The mackerel was cooked in a similar way to the recipe for Spiced Sardines and was absolutely delicious – any oily fish would cook well in this way: herrings in season would make a delicious and very economical dish.

## Pomfret – an Indian Speciality

Pomfret is highly prized in all Eastern cookery and is the ultimate fish for Indian cookery. It is the most extraordinary and distinctive fish to look at, having an almost translucent whiteness to its flesh – on a fishmongers slab, amongst other fish with the more common brown, grey or pinky-orange skins, it shimmers and demands to be noticed. It is a flat fish with a sharply forked tail and distinctive fins, the skin graduating from a shimmering grey to an almost pure white on the belly.

Pomfret has a texture that is similar to turbot and it is often cooked with fresh coriander, chillies and a paste of ginger and garlic. The classic way to cook the fish is by wrapping it in banana leaves before baking or steaming it – aluminium foil just doesn't give the same results.

## Under Rather Than Over

The most important rule when cooking fish is to cook it quickly, so as not to lose all the moisture from the flesh, resulting in a dry, unpalatable dish. It almost takes longer to assemble and prepare the ingredients for the majority of recipes in this chapter than it does to actually cook them! Always under-cook fish rather than over-cook it – it will probably be done to perfection by the time you have served the dish and presented it to your family and friends.

## When is a Duck a Fish?

When it's a Bombay Duck! You will know if you have ever been in close proximity to one of these – the smell is unmistakable! Bombay Duck is dried bombil, a small fish caught in huge quantities in Indian waters, especially off Bombay so hence the name. The fish are dried in the sun and provide a cheap form of protein for many Indian people. In the west, they are served as an accompaniment to curries and other Indian dishes. In India, Bombay Duck often provides all the protein in a meal and, dried or fresh, it is made into many different dishes. You may occasionally get Bombay Duck in a fishmongers, but it is more usually found in an Indian grocers or delicatessen. I find it too strong a flavour, but friends of mine who are addicts run it under cold water and then bake it briefly in the oven to soften the flesh before eating it. It's all a matter of taste!

# PRAWN CHILLI MASALA

*King prawns are favoured for curries in India, but any large frozen prawns may be used in this dish.*

Serves 4

## INGREDIENTS
90g/3oz unsalted butter
6 green cardamoms, split open the top of each pod
2.5cm/1 inch piece of fresh root ginger, peeled and finely grated
3-4 cloves garlic, peeled and crushed
1 tbsp ground coriander
½ tsp ground turmeric
460g/1lb peeled prawns
150ml/¼ pint thick-set natural yogurt
90ml/3 fl oz water
1 tsp sugar
1 tsp salt
30g/1oz ground almonds
4-6 whole fresh green chillies
120g/4oz onions, finely chopped
2 fresh green chillies, seeded and minced
½ tsp garam masala
1 tbsp freshly chopped coriander leaves

Melt 60g/2oz of butter over a gentle heat and add the whole cardamoms; fry for 30 seconds then add the ginger and garlic. Stir and cook for 1 minute, before adding the ground coriander and turmeric. Stir fry for 30 seconds. Add the prawns, increase the heat and cook for 3-4 minutes, stirring frequently.

Beat the yogurt until smooth, gradually adding the water. Add this mixture to the prawns with the sugar and the salt, cover the pan and simmer for 5-6 minutes. Add the ground almonds and the whole green chillies and cook, uncovered, for 5 minutes.

Meanwhile, fry the onions in the remaining butter until they are just soft, but not brown. Add the minced green chillies and the garam masala and cook for a further 1-2 minutes. Stir this mixture into the prawns along with any butter left in the pan. Turn the prawns into a warmed serving dish and garnish with the coriander leaves.

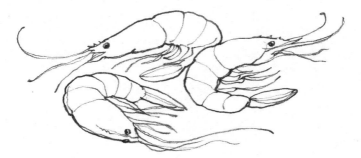

# FISH BHOONA

*A bhoona is a fairly spicy curry, sometimes hot and sometimes medium, cooked in hot oil, which removes any floury dryness from the spices.*

Serves 4

### INGREDIENTS

680g/1½lbs white fish fillets or
 steaks
6 tbsps cooking oil

1 tbsp plain flour
¼ tsp ground turmeric
¼ tsp chilli powder
¼ tsp salt

1 large onion, roughly chopped
1.25cm/½ inch piece of fresh
 root ginger, peeled and
 roughly chopped
2-4 cloves garlic, peeled and
 roughly chopped
½ tsp ground turmeric
¼ tsp chilli powder
1 tsp ground coriander
½ tsp garam masala
200g/7oz can tomatoes
150ml/¼ pint warm water
120g/4oz frozen peas
1 tsp salt
1 tbsp freshly chopped coriander
 leaves

Skin the fish, rinse and dry thoroughly on absorbent kitchen paper, then cut the fish into approximately 2.5 × 5cm/1 × 2 inch pieces. Heat 2 tbsps of the oil in a large frying pan, preferably non-stick or cast iron, over a medium heat. Mix the flour with the seasonings, then lightly dust the fish, one piece at a time, in the seasoned flour and place in the hot oil. Put in as many pieces as the pan will comfortably hold in a single layer. Increase the heat slightly and fry the fish until all the pieces are evenly browned. This has to be done quickly in fairly hot oil so that the fish is thoroughly sealed. Fry all the fish this way and drain on absorbent kitchen paper.

Place the onion, ginger and garlic in a liquidiser or food processor and blend until smooth. Heat the remaining oil in a wide, shallow pan, over a medium heat. Add the onion mixture and cook for 3-4 minutes, reducing the heat as necessary. Add the turmeric, chilli, coriander and garam masala and fry for 4-5 minutes, stirring continuously. Add the juice from the tomatoes, a little at a time, to prevent the spices from sticking to the bottom of the pan. Add the tomatoes and cook for 2-3 minutes, breaking them up with a spoon and mixing them into the other ingredients. Add the water, peas and salt. Bring to the boil and add the fish. Cover and simmer for 5 to 6 minutes. Garnish the bhoona with the coriander leaves and serve.

# COD CURRY

*This is really two recipes in one! It's up to you to decide*
*whether to use yogurt or tomatoes as either one is delicious.*

Serves 4

### INGREDIENTS

3 tbsps vegetable oil
1 large onion, chopped
2.5cm/1 inch piece cinnamon
  stick
1 bay leaf
1.25cm/½ inch piece root ginger,
  peeled and grated
2-3 cloves garlic, peeled and
  crushed
1 tsp chilli powder
1 tsp ground cumin
1 tsp ground coriander
¼ tsp ground turmeric
150ml/¼ pint natural yogurt *or*
  200g/7oz can tomatoes,
  chopped
1-2 fresh green chillies, chopped
1 tbsp freshly chopped coriander
  leaves
460g/1lb cod cutlets, or fillets,
  cut into 5cm/2 inch pieces
1 tsp salt

Fry the onion in the oil in a large
heavy-based saucepan until
golden brown. Add the
cinnamon, bay leaf, ginger and
garlic and fry for 1 minute. Add
the ground spices and fry for a
further minute over a low heat,
then stir in *either* the yogurt *or*
the canned tomatoes and the
chopped chillies and coriander.
Only if you have used yogurt, stir
in 150ml/¼ pint water and
simmer the mixture for 2-3
minutes. Do not add any water if
you have used canned tomatoes.
Stir the cod into the sauce, and
add the salt. Cover the pan and
simmer for 10-15 minutes before
serving.

# TANDOORI FISH

*Firm white fish fillets are ideal for Tandoori Fish, although I have cooked the recipe most successfully using mackerel fillets.*

Serves 4

### INGREDIENTS
460g/1lb white fish fillets or steaks
2 cloves garlic, peeled and roughly chopped
Small piece of fresh root ginger, peeled and coarsely chopped
½ tsp salt
1 tsp ground cumin
1 tsp ground coriander
½ tsp garam masala
¼-½ tsp chilli powder
¼ tsp tandoori colour *or* a few drops of red food colouring mixed with 1 tbsp tomato purée
Juice of ½ lemon
3 tbsps water
2 tbsps cooking oil

2 heaped tbsps flour
½ tsp chilli powder
¼ tsp salt

Rinse the fish and dry on absorbent kitchen paper. Cut into 2.5cm/1 inch squares. Add the salt to the ginger and garlic and crush to a smooth pulp, then mix with the cumin, coriander, garam masala, chilli powder and tandoori colour or tomato purée mix. Add the lemon juice and water and mix thoroughly. Set to one side.

Heat the oil in a non-stick or cast iron frying pan over a medium heat. Mix the flour, chilli powder and salt. Dust each piece of fish in the seasoned flour and put in the hot oil in a single layer – leave plenty of room in the pan. Fry for 5 minutes, turning once, then drain on absorbent kitchen paper. Return all the fish to the pan. Hold a sieve over the pan and pour the liquid spice mixture into it. Press with the back of a metal spoon until only dry waste is left in the sieve – discard. Stir the spices gently into the fish and cook over a medium heat until the fish is fully coated with the spices and the liquid dries up. Serve immediately.

# MASALA MACHCHI

*Masala Machchi is a medium hot, spicy fish dish, strongly flavoured with lemon juice.*

Serves 4

*INGREDIENTS*
Juice of ½ lemon
1 small onion, roughly chopped
2-3 cloves garlic, peeled and
  roughly chopped
2.5cm/1 inch piece of fresh root
  ginger, peeled and roughly
  chopped
1-2 fresh green chillies, chopped;
  seed the chillies if you like a
  milder flavour
3 tbsps freshly chopped
  coriander leaves
1 tsp salt
460g/1lb white fish fillets
90ml/3 fl oz oil for shallow-frying
Lemon slices for garnish

*Coating*
3 tbsps plain flour
1 egg, beaten
¼ tsp salt
¼ tsp chilli powder

Place the lemon juice, onion, garlic, ginger, green chillies, coriander leaves and 1 teaspoon of salt in a liquidiser or food processor and blend until smooth. Rinse the fish and pat dry with absorbent kitchen paper. Cut the fish into 4 × 2.5cm/1½ × 1 inch pieces. Brush a light coating of the spice paste onto all sides of each piece of fish, cover and leave to marinate in a cool place for 2-3 hours, or overnight in the refrigerator.

Mix the flour for frying with the salt and chilli powder. Dust each piece of fish lightly with the mixture, then dip in the beaten egg. Shallow-fry in a single layer over a medium heat until the fish is brown on both sides – 2-3 minutes on each side. Drain on absorbent kitchen paper. Alternatively, deep-fry the fish until golden brown and drain on absorbent kitchen paper. Serve garnished with slices of lemon.

# SPICED SARDINES

*This recipe combines some of my favourite flavours in a lightly spiced curry, especially if served with an avocado chutney.*

Serves 4

### INGREDIENTS

8 fresh sardines (about 680g/1½ lbs)
1 tsp salt
3-4 cloves garlic, peeled and roughly chopped
Juice of ½ lemon
½ tsp ground turmeric
½-1 tsp chilli powder
3 tbsps plain flour
60ml/2 fl oz cooking oil

Scale and clean the fish. Rinse in cold water and dry on absorbent kitchen paper.

Add the salt to the garlic and work to a smooth pulp. Mix all the remaining ingredients together in a small bowl except the fish, flour and oil. Place the fish in a wide shallow dish and pour the marinade over. Spread it gently over both sides of the fish, then cover and refrigerate for 2-4 hours.

Heat the oil over a medium heat. Dip each fish in the flour and coat it thoroughly. Fry until golden brown on both sides – this will take 2-3 minutes per side. Drain on absorbent kitchen paper.

# COD ROE SCRAMBLE

*This highly nutritious dish is lightly spiced, which takes away much of the richness of the roe.*

Serves 4

*INGREDIENTS*
225g/8oz fresh cod roe
2 tbsps cooking oil
1 onion, finely chopped
1 fresh green chilli, finely
   chopped
2 tbsps ground coriander
½ tsp ground turmeric
½ tsp salt

Chop the cod roe roughly. Heat the oil in a non-stick or cast iron pan over a medium heat and fry the onion and green chilli until the onion is soft but not brown. Add the coriander and turmeric, stir, and cook for 1 minute, then add the cod roe and salt. Cook for 3-4 minutes, breaking up the pieces of roe with a spoon. Reduce the heat to low and cook until the roe begins to brown, stirring occasionally. Remove from the heat and serve.

# SPRAT FRY

*The sprats for this starter are fried whole, like whitebait.*

Serves 4

*INGREDIENTS*
225g/8oz cleaned sprats
¼ tsp turmeric
1 tsp chilli powder
1 tsp salt
Oil for deep-frying
Lemon juice

Rub the sprats well with turmeric, chilli powder and salt. Gently heat the oil and fry the fish for 6-8 minutes, a few at a time, until crisp. Drain on absorbent kitchen paper, then sprinkle with lemon juice and serve.

# PRAWN CURRY

*This is a hot, slightly sour prawn curry, delicious with plain boiled rice and a yogurt dressing.*

Serves 4

### INGREDIENTS

1 large onion, chopped
60g/2oz ghee *or* 3 tbsps oil
2.5cm/1 inch cinnamon stick
6 green cardamoms
6 cloves
1 bay leaf
1 tsp fresh root ginger, peeled and grated
2-3 cloves garlic, peeled and crushed
1 tsp chilli powder
1 tsp ground cumin
1 tsp ground coriander
½ tsp salt
1 green pepper, seeded and cut into 1.25cm/½ inch pieces
200g/7oz can tomatoes, crushed
460g/1lb large peeled prawns
1 tbsp freshly chopped coriander leaves
2 green chillies, chopped

Fry the onions in ghee or oil until soft, then add the cinnamon, cardamoms, cloves and bay leaf. Fry for 1 minute and then add ginger and garlic, chilli, cumin, coriander and salt. Fry for 30 seconds. Add the chopped green pepper and tomatoes, then bring to the boil and add the prawns. Return the mixture to the boil and cook for 10-15 minutes. Garnish with the chopped coriander and chopped chillies.

# BENGAL FISH CURRY

*There is an abundance of fish in the Bay of Bengal and the people of this region of India are masters of the art of fish curries.*

Serves 4

### INGREDIENTS
680g/1½lbs firm fleshed fish such as river trout, grey or red mullet
1 tsp ground turmeric
1¼ tsps salt
5 tbsps cooking oil
1 large onion, finely chopped
Small piece of fresh root ginger, peeled and finely chopped or grated
1 tbsp ground coriander
½-1 tsp chilli powder
1 tsp paprika
280ml/½ pint thick-set natural yogurt
4-6 whole fresh green chillies
1-2 cloves of garlic, peeled and crushed
1 tbsp besan (gram or chick pea flour)
2 tbsps freshly chopped coriander leaves

Clean and skin the fish; wash and pat dry. Cut each fish into 4cm/1½ inch pieces, and remove as many bones as possible. Gently rub a little of the turmeric and salt from the specified amounts over the fish, then leave it for 15-20 minutes.

Meanwhile, heat the oil over a medium heat in a pan wide enough to hold the fish in a single layer. Fry the onion and ginger until the onions are lightly browned, stirring frequently. Add the coriander, remaining turmeric, chilli powder and the paprika, reduce the heat to low and cook for 1-2 minutes, stirring continuously. Beat the yogurt with a fork until smooth and add to the pan with the whole green chillies, the remaining salt and the garlic. Increase the heat slightly and mix well. Arrange the pieces of fish in the pan in a single layer and bring to a gentle boil. Cover, and cook over a low heat for 5-6 minutes.

Blend the besan with a little water to give a pouring consistency. Strain the mixture into the fish curry, stir gently to mix. Cover and cook for 2-3 minutes. Remove the pan from the heat and gently mix in half the coriander leaves. Transfer the fish curry to a warmed serving dish and garnish with the remaining coriander leaves.

# FISH SHAHJAHANI

*This rich fish curry is named after the gourmet Mughal Emperor Shahjahan, widely acknowledged for his love of good food. Serve with a plain or mildly flavoured rice.*

Serves 4

### INGREDIENTS

680g/1½lbs white fish fillets
90g/3oz roasted cashews
120ml/4 fl oz single cream
60g/2oz unsalted butter
225g/8oz onions, finely sliced
5cm/2 inch piece of cinnamon
    stick, broken up
4 green cardamoms, the top of
    each pod split open
2 whole cloves
1-2 fresh green chillies, sliced
    lengthways; seeded if a milder
    flavour is preferred
1 tsp ground turmeric
175ml/6 fl oz warm water
1 tsp salt
1 tbsp lemon juice

Rinse the fish in cold water, dry on absorbent kitchen paper and cut into 2.5 × 5cm/1 × 2 inch pieces. Place the cashews and cream in a liquidiser or food processor and blend to a paste.

Melt the butter in a wide, shallow pan over a medium heat and fry the onions, cinnamon, cardamom, cloves and green chillies until the onions are lightly browned. Stir in the turmeric, then add the water and salt and arrange the fish in a single layer. Bring to the boil, then cover the pan and simmer for 2-3 minutes. Add the cashew paste and stir gently until all the pieces of fish are well coated. Cover the pan again and simmer for a further 2-3 minutes. Gently stir in the lemon juice before serving.

# CHICKEN

Chickens are popular the world over. They blend well with so many flavourings, are quick to cook and succulent – well, that would be a fair description of the chickens of the west. Murghi, their Indian cousins, are not of the same quality and are often quite scrawny, although they do have lots of free-range flavour. Chickens are survivors and in many countries they are left to scratch around for their food in the fields and, indeed, in towns. Progress dictates that battery farming will be introduced in most countries before too long and some chicken farms now exist in India, producing better birds for eating. These farms are for both chickens and eggs and it is interesting to note that some vegetarians who would previously not eat eggs will now do so as the farmed eggs are unfertilised.

## Classic Dishes from North and South

Chicken plays an important rôle in just about every great classic cuisine. Some of the best known Indian chicken dishes come from opposite ends of the country. Unless Indians are vegetarian there are no religious reasons to prevent them from eating chicken. The only problem may be that it is too expensive for everyday dishes – for many people chicken is an expensive treat.

Some of the best-known of all Indian dishes originate in the Punjab region of northern India, the home of the tandoor oven. The Punjabis are the cooks and gourmets of India and their tandoori dishes are known throughout the world. Tandoori chicken is always marinated in a mixture of spices and yogurt and the best results are obtained when the meat is marinated overnight. The secret of successful tandoori cooking is a very quick bake in a hot tandoor, a clay oven. It is difficult to reproduce the exact flavour and texture of the tandoor at home, but a reasonable attempt may be made by cooking in a gas or electric oven at its highest temperature. Chicken baked in a tandoor is succulent and juicy on the inside but has a dry, slightly crusty outer surface. Naan breads, one of the few leavened breads of India made with yeast, are cooked in the same oven – the Punjabis eat far more bread than the people of the south as the north is wheat and not rice country.

## Creamy Kormas from the South

One of the best dishes to cook when first introducing friends or family to Indian cookery is a korma, a mild creamy dish with yogurt and cream in the sauce, and which is often thickened with ground almonds and seasoned with saffron. A well-made korma is truly a gourmet's delight. Such dishes originate in the south of India and are more commonly served with rice than breads, although pieces of chappati are excellent for scooping up all the delicious sauce. I frequently put a tablespoon or so of blue poppy seeds in a korma – I love the nutty texture and extra colour that they give to the sauce.

Some people cook lamb or mutton as a korma but I never feel that this is as successful as chicken – the white meat complements the creamy sauce more readily and naturally.

## Other Poultry and Game Birds

Chicken is not the only bird to enjoy a place in the classic cooking of India – duck and goose are also eaten but are reserved for special occasions. Of the game birds, partridge is a special favourite, reserved for the grandest of celebrations. Chicken is really the only poultry to be eaten in any quantity and for many of the people of India even that is a luxury.

Chicken is one of the few major ingredients that really works well with almost any seasonings or ingredients. I have been lyrical about the mildest of curries, the korma and the gourmet dishes of the tandoor but I should say that chicken cooks just as well as a vindaloo, a very hot sour curry cooked with a little vinegar to give a unique (and tongue tingling) flavour. A flick through this chapter will reveal recipes for Masalas, Makkhani (a very rich butter sauce), and Kohlapuri, a hot chilli based recipe from the south of India. The recipe for Chicken Chaat, in which the chicken pieces are very lightly spiced and stir-fried, is one of the simplest of Indian recipes and is every bit as delightful as some of the more complicated dishes. Such is the versatility of chicken.

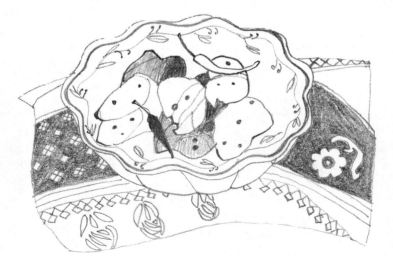

# CORIANDER CHICKEN

*This is a good curry to serve at an Indian dinner party. After the chicken has been marinated the curry cooks quickly and requires little attention. Garnish with fresh coriander leaf for extra flavour.*

Serves 6

### INGREDIENTS

6 chicken joints, skinned
2-4 cloves garlic, peeled and crushed
150ml/¼ pint thick-set natural yogurt
5 tbsps cooking oil
1 large onion, finely sliced
2 tbsps ground coriander
½ tsp ground black pepper
1 tsp ground mixed spice
½ tsp ground turmeric
½ tsp cayenne pepper or chilli powder
120ml/4 fl oz warm water
1 tsp salt
30g/1oz ground almonds
2 hard-boiled eggs, sliced
¼ tsp paprika

Cut each chicken joint into two, add the crushed garlic and the yogurt and stir. Cover and leave to marinate in a cool place for 2-4 hours or overnight in the refrigerator.

Heat the oil in a large pan over a medium heat and fry the onions until they are golden brown. Remove them with a slotted spoon and set to one side. Fry the coriander, ground pepper, ground mixed spice and turmeric for 15 seconds then add the chicken in the same oil, with all the marinade. Fry the chicken over a medium heat for 5-6 minutes until it changes colour. Add the cayenne or chilli powder, water, salt, and the reserved fried onions. Bring to the boil, cover the pan and simmer until the chicken is tender, about 30 minutes. Stir in the ground almonds. Garnish the curry with the sliced hard-boiled eggs and paprika, and chopped coriander leaf, if required.

# MURGHI AUR ALOO

*Murghi aur aloo is a classic Parsi dish, showing the influence of this ancient Persian people on classic Indian cookery.*

Serves 4-6

### INGREDIENTS

1kg/2¼lbs chicken joints, skinned
1½ tsps salt
2.5cm/1 inch piece of fresh root ginger, peeled and roughly chopped
4-6 cloves garlic, peeled and roughly chopped

*Whole spices*
2 tsps cumin seeds
4-6 dried red chillies
2 brown cardamoms, seeds only, *or* 4 green cardamoms
6 whole cloves
2 cinnamon sticks, 5cm/2 inches long, broken up into 2-3 pieces
6 black peppercorns

1 tbsp white poppy seeds
10 raw whole cashews

4 tbsps cold water
60g/2oz ghee or unsalted butter
30g/1oz fresh coriander leaves and stalks, finely chopped
1-2 fresh green chillies, cut into halves lengthways, seeded if a milder flavour is preferred
½ tsp ground turmeric

280ml/½ pint warm water
½ tsp saffron strands
460g/1lb potatoes, peeled and quartered
150ml/¼ pint soured cream
2-3 hard-boiled eggs, cut into quarters

Cut each chicken joint into two; separate legs from thighs and cut each breast into two pieces. Add the salt to the ginger and garlic and crush them to a pulp. Grind the whole spices, then grind the poppy seeds and cashews together. Mix the ground ingredients, including the poppy seeds and cashews, into a thick paste by adding the cold water. Break up any lumps with the back of a spoon and then set the paste aside.

Melt the ghee or butter over a low heat and add the ginger and garlic paste. Cook for 2-3 minutes, stirring continuously. Add the spice paste, stir and cook for 2-3 minutes, then add the chicken and increase the heat to medium-high. Fry the chicken until it changes colour in 5-6 minutes. Add the coriander leaves, green chillies and turmeric, stir and fry for a further 2-3 minutes, then add the water. Bring to the boil and add the saffron strands, then cover and simmer for 15 minutes.

Add the potatoes to the pan and cook for a further 20 minutes or until the chicken and the potatoes are tender and the sauce is fairly thick. Beat the soured cream until smooth and stir it into the chicken. Cook, uncovered, for 6-8 minutes stirring frequently. Arrange the chicken curry in a warmed serving dish and garnish with the hard-boiled egg quarters.

# MAKKHANI MURGHI

*This is a rich chicken curry in a butter sauce – it is quite an unusual dish and is certainly suitable for serving at a dinner party.*

Serves 6-8

*Ingredients*

*Ingredients*
1kg/2¼lbs boneless chicken breast, skinned
1¼ tsps salt
2.5cm/1 inch piece of fresh root ginger, peeled and roughly chopped
4-6 cloves garlic, peeled and roughly chopped

150g/5oz thick-set natural yogurt
Juice of 1 lemon

*Whole Spices*
1 cinnamon stick, 2 inches long, broken up
8 green cardamoms
6 whole cloves
8-10 red chillies
6-8 white peppercorns

2 tbsps cooking oil
2 tbsps tomato purée
225g/8oz butter
400g/14oz can tomatoes
2 cinnamon sticks, 5cm/2 inches long, broken up
150ml/¼ pint single cream

Cut the chicken into strips, 5 × 10cm/2 × 4 inches. Add the salt to the ginger and garlic and crush to a smooth pulp. Grind the whole spices. Combine the yogurt, lemon juice and the ground spices and beat until the mixture is smooth. Marinate the chicken in this mixture, cover, and leave in a cool place for 2-4 hours or overnight in the refrigerator.

Heat the oil over a medium heat and add the ginger and garlic pulp, stir and fry for 1 minute. Add the chicken and fry for 10 minutes, stirring frequently. Add the tomato purée and butter, and cook over a low heat, uncovered, for 10 minutes. Remove the pan from the heat, cover and leave on one side.

Place the tomatoes and cinnamon sticks in a separate pan, bring to the boil, cover and simmer for 10 minutes. Remove the lid and cook uncovered over a medium heat, until the liquid is reduced by half. Remove the pan from the heat and allow the tomato mixture to cool slightly, then sieve the cooked tomatoes, and discard the cinnamon sticks. Add the sieved tomatoes to the chicken and place the pan over a medium heat. Bring to the boil, reduce the heat to low and cook, uncovered, for 5-6 minutes. Add the cream, stir and simmer uncovered for about 5 minutes, then serve.

# SPICED ORIENTAL CHICKEN

*This unusual method of cooking chickens has them dusted with mixed spices just before serving.*

Serves 6-8

## INGREDIENTS

2 × 1.15-1.4kg/2½lb-3lb chickens, skinned
10 dried curry leaves, crumbled
¾-1 tsp cayenne pepper
2 tsps ground coriander
1 tsp ground cumin
2-3 green chillies, finely chopped
5cm/2 inch piece fresh root ginger, peeled and finely chopped
1 cinnamon stick, broken into pieces
1 tsp turmeric
5 cloves garlic, peeled and finely chopped
2 bay leaves, crumbled
2 tsps salt
2 Spanish onions, finely chopped
6 tbsps vegetable oil
225ml/8 fl oz coconut milk
1 tsp sugar
2 tsps lime juice

## Garnish
½ tsp ground coriander
½ tsp garam masala
¼ tsp freshly ground cloves
½ tsp freshly ground cardamom seeds
½ tsp ground cinnamon

Prick the chickens all over with a fork. Mix together the curry leaves, cayenne, coriander, cumin, chilli, ginger, cinnamon, turmeric, garlic, bay leaves, salt, onions and vegetable oil. Rub the mixture all over the skinned chickens in a large bowl. Cover with plastic wrap, then allow to marinate overnight in a cool place.

Brown the chickens in the marinade in a large flameproof casserole. Add the coconut milk, cover, and simmer gently until the chicken is tender, in about 45-60 minutes. Remove the chickens from the casserole and keep them warm.

Add the sugar to the casserole juices and boil to reduce the liquid a little, then stir in the lime juice and pour this sauce over the chickens.

Mix the remaining spices together and sprinkle them over the chickens just before serving.

# LIME AND CORIANDER CHICKEN

*Coriander and chicken make a perfect combination,*
*especially if served with saffron scented rice.*

Serves 6

*INGREDIENTS*

1.8 kg/4 lb chicken, skinned (or 2 small chickens)
2 tbsps lime or lemon juice
½ tsp salt
2-3 fresh green chillies, very finely chopped
1 bunch freshly chopped coriander leaves (with roots and lower stems removed)
¼ tsp cayenne pepper
5cm/2 inch piece fresh root ginger, peeled and finely chopped
6 tbsps natural yogurt
6 cloves garlic, peeled and crushed
2 tbsps vegetable oil
Fresh coriander leaves and lime or lemon wedges for garnish

Prick the chicken all over with a fork. Combine the lime or lemon juice, salt and chilli in a large bowl and rub the mixture over the chicken. Set to one side whilst the marinade is prepared. Place the coriander, cayenne pepper, ginger and yogurt in a bowl and mix well. Add the marinade to the chicken, coating the chicken all over. Cover the bowl with plastic wrap and leave for at least 6 hours.

Preheat the oven to 200°C/400°F/Gas Mark 6. Place the vegetable oil in a roasting tin with the chicken and marinade mixture. Bake the chicken in the centre of the oven for 20 minutes, then reduce the oven temperature to 180°C/350°F/Gas Mark 4 and continue baking for about 45 minutes or until the chicken is tender. The chicken should be regularly basted with the pan juices.

Skim any fat from the pan juices with a spoon. Place the chicken on a hot serving plate, spoon the sauce over and serve immediately, garnished with the fresh coriander leaves and wedges of lime or lemon.

# MURGHI BADAMI

*I've always thought of chicken korma as a fairly rich,
creamy dish, but this is a richer korma, cooked entirely in
yogurt and cream. A succulent dish!*

Serves 4-6

### INGREDIENTS
1kg/2¼lbs chicken joints,
  skinned
1 tsp salt
2.5cm/1 inch piece of fresh root
  ginger, peeled and chopped
3-4 cloves garlic, peeled and
  chopped
1 tsp freshly ground black
  pepper
1 tbsp lemon juice
280g/10oz thick-set natural
  yogurt
60g/2oz ghee or unsalted butter
2 onions, finely sliced
6 green cardamoms, the top of
  each pod split open
1 tbsp ground coriander
1 tsp ground turmeric
150ml/¼ pint single cream
¼-½ tsp chilli powder
60g/2oz flaked almonds
1 tbsp ground almonds

Cut each chicken joint into two –
separate legs from thighs and cut
each breast into two pieces.
Make small incisions on both
sides of the chicken pieces with
a sharp knife. This is to allow the
spices to penetrate the flesh
deeply. Add the salt to the ginger
and garlic and crush to a fine
pulp. Mix with the pepper and
lemon juice, then rub this
mixture into the chicken, cover
and leave for 30-60 minutes. Beat
the yogurt until smooth and set
to one side.

Melt the ghee or butter over a
medium heat and fry the onions
until well browned. Remove the
pan from the heat and squeeze
out any excess fat by pressing
the onions to the side of the pan.
Transfer the onions to a plate.
Return the pan to the heat and
add the cardamoms and
coriander. Stir and fry for 30
seconds, then add the chicken.
Increase the heat to medium-high
and fry the chicken until it
changes colour in 5-6 minutes,
stirring continuously. Stir in the
turmeric and the yogurt, cover
the pan and simmer for 15
minutes, stirring occasionally.

Reserve 2 tbsps of the fried
onions and add the rest to the
chicken with the cream, chilli
powder and flaked almonds, stir
and mix well. Cover and simmer
for a further 15-20 minutes,
stirring occasionally. Add the
ground almonds and mix well,
cover and simmer for a further 6-
8 minutes. Transfer the chicken
to a warmed serving dish and
garnish with the remaining fried
onions.

# INDIAN CHICKEN

*This recipe is for a spiced chicken to cook on the barbecue.
Preheat the oven to 180°C/350°F/Gas Mark 4 if you prefer to
cook the chicken conventionally.*

Serves 4-6

*INGREDIENTS*
1.4kg/3lb chicken, cut into 8
  joints
570ml/1 pint natural yogurt
2 tsps ground coriander
2 tsps paprika
1 tsp ground turmeric
Juice of 1 lime
1 tbsp honey
½ clove garlic, peeled and
  crushed
1 small piece fresh root ginger,
  peeled and grated

Prick the chicken all over with a
fork or skewer. Combine all the
remaining ingredients and spread
half the mixture over the
chicken, rubbing it in well. Place
the chicken in a shallow dish,
cover and leave for at least 4
hours or overnight in the
refrigerator.

If your barbecue has adjustable
shelves, place the cooking rack
on the level furthest from the
coals. Arrange the chicken skin
side down and grill until lightly
browned, turn over and cook the
second side until lightly
browned. Baste frequently with
the remaining marinade. Lower
the grid for the last 15 minutes
and cook, turning and basting
frequently, until the chicken is
brown and the skin is crisp.
Alternatively, cook the chicken in
a covered dish in the oven at
180°C/350°F/Gas Mark 4 for 45
minutes to 1 hour, then grill for a
further 15 minutes to crisp the
skin.

# MURGHI DILKUSH

*Dilkush sounds a little like delicious – a good description of this aromatic chicken curry. Use a pestle and mortar or a coffee grinder to grind the roasted spices and nuts.*

Serves 6-9

## INGREDIENTS

5cm/2 inch piece cinnamon stick, broken up
6 green cardamoms
6 whole cloves
1 tsp cumin seeds
2-3 dried red chillies
1 tbsp channa dhal or yellow split peas

30g/1oz raw cashews
1 tbsp white poppy seeds
1.15kg/2½lbs chicken joints, skin removed
60g/2oz ghee or unsalted butter
2 onions, finely chopped
2.5cm/1 inch piece of fresh root ginger, peeled and roughly chopped
4-6 cloves garlic, peeled and roughly chopped
150g/5oz thick-set natural yogurt

1 tsp garam masala
150ml/5 fl oz warm water
1¼ tsps salt or to taste
25g/1 oz fresh coriander leaves, finely chopped
1 tbsp fresh mint leaves, finely chopped *or* 1 tsp dried or bottled mint
1-2 fresh green chillies, seeded and coarsely chopped

Roast the whole spices and dhal over a low heat until fragrant. Allow to cool then grind. Roast the cashews and poppy seeds together in a similar way until lightly browned and grind when cool.

Cut each chicken joint into two, separate legs from thighs and cut each breast into two. Melt 30g/1oz of ghee over a medium heat and fry the onions, ginger and garlic for 4-5 minutes. Squeeze out excess ghee by pressing the onions onto the side of the pan with a wooden spoon, then transfer the onions to a plate. Allow to cool slightly.

Place the yogurt in a liquidiser or food processor and add all the roasted and ground ingredients and the fried onions. Blend until smooth. Rub this marinade into the chicken pieces and pour over any remaining marinade – mix thoroughly and leave for 4-6 hours or overnight in the refrigerator.

Melt the remaining ghee over a low heat and add the garam masala, stir and fry for 30 seconds. Add the marinated chicken, increase the heat to medium-high and fry for 5-6 minutes, stirring frequently. Add the water and salt, bring to the boil, cover and simmer until the chicken is tender, in 35-40 minutes. Increase the heat to medium, add the fresh coriander, mint and green chillies – stir and fry for 5 minutes, then serve with a pilau rice.

# CHICKEN MOGHLAI WITH CORIANDER CHUTNEY

*A delicious dish of creamy chicken with a spicy chutney or sauce. Use half parsley and half coriander if you prefer, but the flavour of the chutney will not be quite so bright.*

Serves 4-6

### INGREDIENTS
4 tbsps oil
1.4kg/3lbs chicken pieces, skinned
1 tsp ground cardamom seeds
½ tsp ground cinnamon
1 bay leaf
4 cloves
2 onions, finely chopped
2.5cm/1 inch piece fresh root ginger, peeled and grated
4 cloves garlic, peeled and crushed
30g/1oz ground almonds
2 tsps cumin seeds
Pinch of cayenne pepper
280ml/½ pint double cream
6 tbsps natural yogurt
2 tbsps roasted cashew nuts
2 tbsps sultanas
Salt

*Chutney*
90g/3oz fresh coriander leaves
1 green fresh chilli, seeded and chopped
1 tbsp lemon juice
Salt and freshly ground black pepper
Pinch of sugar
1 tbsp oil
½ tsp ground coriander

To prepare the chicken, heat the oil in a large frying pan. Fry the chicken pieces on all sides until golden brown. Remove the chicken with a slotted spoon and set aside. Add the cardamom, cinnamon, bay leaf and cloves to the hot oil and meat juices and fry for 30 seconds. Stir in the onions and fry until soft but not brown. Stir the ginger, garlic, almonds, cumin and cayenne pepper. Cook gently for 2-3 minutes, then stir in the cream. Return the chicken pieces to the pan, along with any juices. Cover and simmer gently for 30-40 minutes, or until the chicken is cooked and tender.

Whilst the chicken is cooking, prepare the chutney. Place the coriander leaves, chilli, lemon, seasonings and sugar into a liquidiser or food processor and blend to a paste. Heat the oil and cook the ground coriander for 1 minute. Add to the processed coriander leaves and blend thoroughly.

Just before serving, stir the yogurt, cashews and sultanas into the chicken. Heat through just enough to plump up the sultanas, but do not allow the mixture to boil. Serve at once with the coriander chutney.

# MURGHI MUSALLAM

*This is an elegant dish of small chickens or poussins, stuffed
and served with pilau rice. A spiced yogurt is used to
marinade the chicken and to make a sauce.*

Serves 4

*INGREDIENTS*

2 spring chickens or poussins,
each weighing about 460g/1lb

*Whole spices*
2 tbsps white poppy seeds
2 tbsps sesame seeds
10 black peppercorns
4 green cardamoms
2-4 dried red chillies

150g/5oz thick-set natural yogurt
2½ tsps salt
½ tsp ground turmeric
1 tbsp ground coriander
90g/3oz ghee or unsalted butter
2 onions, finely sliced

2-3 cloves garlic, peeled and
finely chopped
2 cinnamon sticks, 5cm/2 inches
long, broken up
6 green cardamoms, the top of
each pod split open
4 whole cloves
275g/10oz basmati rice, washed
and soaked in cold water for
30 minutes
570ml/1 pint water
½ tsp saffron strands
2 tbsps ghee or unsalted butter
1 onion, finely chopped
2-4 cloves garlic, peeled and
crushed

Remove the skin and the giblets from the chickens. With a sharp knife, make several slits all over each chicken (do not forget the thighs and the back). Grind the whole spices and mix with the yogurt. Add 1 tsp salt, the turmeric and coriander. Rub half of this mixture into the chickens, making sure that the spices are rubbed deep into the slits. Put the chickens in a deep container, cover and leave for 1 hour.

Meanwhile cook the pilau rice. Melt the 90g/3oz ghee or butter over a medium heat and fry the sliced onions, chopped garlic, cinnamon, cardamoms and cloves, until the onions are lightly browned. Add the rice, stir and fry until all the moisture evaporates in 4-5 minutes. Add the remaining salt, water and saffron strands. Bring to the boil, cover the pan and simmer until the rice has absorbed all the water in 12-14 minutes. Do not lift the lid or stir the rice during cooking. Remove the pan from the heat and leave it undisturbed for about 10 minutes.

Using a metal spoon, carefully transfer about a quarter of the cooked rice to a plate and allow it to cool. Keep the remaining rice covered. Stuff each chicken with as much of the cooled pilau rice as the cavity will hold. Truss the chickens as for roasting, so that the rice stays enclosed while the stuffed chicken is being braised.

Melt the 2 tbsps of ghee or butter in a cast iron or nonstick pan. Add the chopped onion and the crushed garlic, stir and fry for 2-3 minutes. Place the chicken on the bed of onions, on their backs, along with any marinade left in the container, but not the marinade which has been reserved. Cover the pan and cook for 10 minutes; turn the chicken over, breast side down, cover and cook for a further 10 minutes. Turn the chickens on their backs again and spread the remaining marinade evenly on each chicken. Cover the pan and cook for a further 30 minutes, turning the chickens over every 10 minutes.

Put the chickens on a warmed serving dish and spread a little sauce evenly over the breast. Spoon the remaining sauce round the chickens. Serve the remaining pilau rice separately, reheating it if necessary.

# CHICKEN LIVER MASALA

*The Muslims are particularly fond of liver curries – this Masala is quite hot and might be served with chapatties and chutney.*

Serves 4

### INGREDIENTS
460g/1lb chicken livers
4 tbsps cooking oil
1 large onion, finely chopped
1 cinnamon stick, 5cm/2 inches long, broken up
225g/8oz potatoes, peeled and diced
1¼ tsps salt
90ml/3 fl oz warm water
3-4 cloves garlic, peeled and crushed

*Spice Paste*
2 tsps ground coriander
1 tsp ground cumin
1 tsp ground turmeric
½ tsp chilli powder
2 tsps water

200g/7oz can tomatoes
120g/4oz frozen peas
2-3 fresh whole green chillies
½ tsp garam masala

Clean the livers, and cut into 1.25cm/½ inch pieces. Heat 2 tbsps of oil over a medium heat and fry the onion and cinnamon stick until the onion is soft. Add the potatoes and ¼ tsp of salt, then stir fry the potatoes for about 2 minutes. Add the water, cover the pan and simmer until the potatoes are tender.

Meanwhile, heat the remaining oil over a medium heat in a heavy-based, wide pan. A nonstick or cast iron pan is ideal as the liver needs to be stir-fried over high heat. Add the garlic and stir-fry for 30 seconds. Mix the ground spices to a paste with the water. Add the spice paste to the pan, reduce the heat to low and fry for about 2 minutes. Add half the tomatoes, with some of the juice, stir and cook for a further 2-3 minutes, breaking up the tomatoes with a spoon. When the mixture is fairly dry, add the livers and increase the heat to medium-high. Stir-fry the livers for 3-4 minutes. Add the remaining tomatoes and the juice, and fry for 5-6 minutes. Cover the pan and simmer for a further 6-8 minutes.

Add the cooked potatoes, peas, green chillies and the remaining salt and cook for 1-2 minutes. Reduce the heat to medium and cook, uncovered, for a further 4-5 minutes. Stir in the garam masala and serve.

# CHICKEN LIVERS WITH SPINACH

*I don't immediately think of making curry with chicken livers, but this sounds like a delicious dish of livers and spinach.*

Serves 4-6

## INGREDIENTS

460g/1lb chicken livers
1¼ tsps salt
2-3 cloves garlic, peeled
120g/4oz frozen leaf spinach
   (defrosted and drained), *or*
   340g/12oz fresh spinach
   roughly chopped
5 tbsps cooking oil
1 tsp ground turmeric
1½ tsps ground coriander
1 tsp ground cumin
¼-½ tsp chilli powder
¼ tsp black mustard seeds
1 tsp cumin seeds
1 large onion, finely sliced
½ tsp garam masala
½ small red pepper, seeded, and
   cut into matchstick strips

Clean the livers, remove any tubes and cut into 2.5cm/1 inch pieces. Wash and drain thoroughly, and dry on absorbent kitchen paper. Add the salt to the garlic and crush to a pulp, using a pestle and mortar, or the blade of a knife.

Heat 2 tbsps of oil over a medium heat. When the oil is smoking hot, carefully add the chicken livers, spread them quickly and cover the pan. Cook for 6-8 minutes, stir once or twice, then remove the lid and cook off any excess liquid. Add the garlic pulp, lower the heat and stir-fry the garlic for 2-3 minutes. Add the turmeric, coriander, cumin and chilli powder; stir and mix well. Cook the livers, uncovered, over a low heat for 4-5 minutes, stirring occasionally.

Heat the remaining oil over medium heat in a separate pan and add the mustard seeds. As soon as they pop, add the cumin seeds followed by the onion. Stir and fry the onion until golden brown. Add the garam masala and the red pepper and stir-fry for 1-2 minutes, then add the spinach, increase the heat to medium-high and stir-fry the spinach for 2-3 minutes.

Add the spinach to the livers with any juices left in the pan. Reduce the heat to low, stir and fry the spinach and the livers for 1-2 minutes. Cook, uncovered, for a further 4-5 minutes, stirring occasionally. Serve with bread or rice.

# TANDOORI CHICKEN

*One of the best-known and most popular restaurant curries, tandoori chicken really requires a tandoor oven. It generates a particularly fierce heat, giving a lightly crusty surface to the chicken, but leaving it moist on the inside. Gas or electric ovens, used on their highest setting, give an acceptable result but the chicken lacks the clay-cooked flavour achieved in a tandoor.*

Serves 6

*INGREDIENTS*
6 chicken joints
1 tsp salt
Juice of ½ lemon
1.25cm/½ inch piece of fresh root ginger, peeled and roughly chopped
2-3 small cloves of garlic, peeled and roughly chopped
1 fresh green chilli, roughly chopped and seeded if a milder flavour is preferred
2 tbsps freshly chopped coriander leaves
90g/3 fl oz thick-set natural yogurt
1 tsp ground coriander
½ tsp ground cumin
1 tsp garam masala
¼ tsp freshly ground black pepper
½ tsp tandoori colour, *or* a few drops of red food colouring mixed with 1 tbsp tomato purée

Remove the skin from the chicken and cut each piece into two. Make 2-3 slits in each piece, and rub salt and lemon juice into the chicken pieces, then set aside for half an hour. Meanwhile, put the ginger, garlic, green chilli, coriander leaves and yogurt in a liquidiser or food processor and blend until smooth. Add the remaining ingredients and blend again. Spread the marinade all over the chicken, especially into the slits. Cover the container and leave the chicken to marinate for 6-8 hours or overnight in the refrigerator.

Preheat oven to 240°C/475°F/Gas Mark 9. Line a roasting tin with aluminium foil (this will help to maintain the high level of heat required to cook the chicken) and arrange the chicken pieces in it. Place the roasting tin in the centre of the oven and bake for 25-30 minutes, turning the pieces over carefully as they brown and basting with the juice in the roasting tin as well as any remaining marinade. Shake any excess liquid off the chicken and serve immediately with a salad garnish.

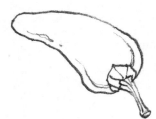

# TANDOORI CHICKEN MASALA

*A masala is a mixture of spices. This popular chicken curry is flavoured with saffron, cardamom and cinnamon.*

Serves 4-6

## INGREDIENTS

1kg/2¼lbs cooked Tandoori Chicken (see recipe)
60g/2oz ghee or unsalted butter
1 large onion, finely chopped
1.25cm/½ inch piece of fresh root ginger, peeled and crushed
2 cloves garlic, peeled and crushed
1 tsp ground cardamom seeds
1 tsp ground cinnamon
¼ tsp chilli powder
1 tsp salt
150ml/¼ pint soured cream
225ml/8 fl oz warm stock (made up of the reserved cooking liquid from the chicken and warm water)
4 tbsps ground almonds
2 tbsps milk
½ tsp saffron strands
30g/1oz toasted flaked almonds

Heat the ghee or butter over a low heat and fry the onion until just soft, but not brown. Add the ginger and garlic and fry for two minutes, stirring constantly, then add the cardamom, cinnamon, chilli powder and salt and fry for 1 minute, stirring constantly.

Beat the soured cream with a fork until smooth, adding half the stock while beating. Add this mixture to the onions and bring to a slow simmer. Add the remaining stock, cover the pan and simmer for 10 minutes. Stir the ground almonds into the mixture then remove the pan from the heat.

Heat the milk and soak the saffron strands in it for 10-15 minutes.

Arrange the tandoori chicken in a wide shallow pan. Blend the onion and cream mixture in a liquidiser or food processor until smooth, then pour the purée over the chicken, then pour the saffron milk and all the saffron strands evenly into the pan. Place the pan over a gentle heat and bring the liquid to boiling point. Cover the pan and simmer for 15 minutes or until heated through, turning the chicken once or twice. Place the chicken in a serving dish and garnish with the toasted almonds.

# MURGHI NAWABI

*Murghal cuisine from which this recipe originates, is delicately flavoured and dressed with rich, velvety sauces. Allow the coconut flavour to dominate the dish.*

Serves 4

### INGREDIENTS
4 large chicken breasts, skinned
150ml/¼ pint thick-set natural yogurt
½ tsp ground turmeric
3-4 cloves garlic, peeled and coarsely chopped
2.5cm/1 inch piece of fresh root ginger, peeled and roughly chopped
4-6 dried red chillies
60g/2oz ghee or unsalted butter
2 large onions, finely sliced
1 tsp caraway seeds
1 tsp garam masala
1¼ tsps salt
225ml/8 fl oz warm water plus 90ml/3 fl oz cold water
100g/3½oz creamed coconut, cut into small pieces
90g/3oz raw cashews
2 hard-boiled eggs, sliced
¼ tsp paprika

Cut each chicken breast into two pieces. Wash the chicken and dry on absorbent kitchen paper. Beat the yogurt and turmeric together until smooth then add to the chicken and mix thoroughly. Cover and leave to marinate for 4-6 hours or overnight in the refrigerator.

Place the garlic, ginger and red chillies in a liquidiser or food processor and add just enough water to allow the ingredients to blend until smooth. Alternatively, crush the garlic and ginger and finely chop the chillies.

Melt the ghee or butter over a medium heat and fry the onions until they are brown. Remove the pan from heat and, using a wooden spatula, press the onions to the side of the pan in order to squeeze out any excess fat. Transfer the onions to a plate and set aside. Return the pan to the heat and fry the caraway seeds and garam masala for 30 seconds, then add the blended garlic, ginger and chillies. Stir briskly and add the chicken, fried onions and salt. Cook for 5-6 minutes, stirring frequently and lowering heat as the chicken is heated through. Add any remaining yogurt marinade to the chicken, then the water and the creamed coconut. Bring to the boil, cover the pan and simmer until the chicken is tender and the sauce is thick, in about 30-35 minutes. Stir occasionally.

Meanwhile, place the cashews in a blender or food processor, add the cold water and blend until smooth. Add the cashew paste to the chicken during the last 5 minutes of cooking time. Simmer uncovered for 4-5 minutes, stirring frequently. Place the chicken in a warmed serving dish and garnish with the sliced eggs. Garnish with the paprika.

# CHICKEN CHAAT

*This lightly spiced, stir-fried curry may be served as a main course with salad garnish or on cocktail sticks as a drinks party savoury. Serve as a main course with sliced raw onion and cucumber.*

Serves 4

*INGREDIENTS*
680g/1½lbs chicken breast, skinned and boned
1 tsp salt
2-3 cloves garlic, peeled and roughly chopped
2 tbsps cooking oil
1½ tsps ground coriander
¼ tsp ground turmeric
¼-½ tsp chilli powder
1½ tbsps lemon juice
2 tbsps freshly chopped coriander leaves

Wash the chicken and dry on absorbent kitchen paper. Cut into 2.5cm/1 inch cubes. Add the salt to the garlic and crush to a smooth pulp. Heat the oil in a frying pan, preferably non-stick or cast iron, over medium heat, then add the garlic and fry until it is lightly browned. Add the chicken and fry for 6-7 minutes, stirring constantly. Add the ground coriander, turmeric and chilli powder. Fry for 3-4 minutes, stirring frequently. Remove from heat and stir in the lemon juice and coriander leaves. Serve hot or cold.

# SABJI MASALA MURGHI

*This medium-spiced chicken curry is cooked with plenty of vegetables in the sauce, so I would suggest just serving rice or bread, pickles and raita with it.*

Serves 4

### INGREDIENTS

4 large chicken breasts
200ml/7 fl oz water
90g/3oz roasted cashews
60g/2oz ghee or unsalted butter
2.5cm/1 inch piece of fresh root ginger, peeled and finely grated
4-6 cloves garlic, peeled and finely chopped

*Spices*
¼ tsp ground nutmeg
6 green cardamoms
1 tsp caraway seeds
4-6 dried red chillies

1¼ tsps salt
60g/2oz whole baby carrots
60g/2oz frozen garden peas
60g/2oz frozen sweetcorn
4 spring onions, roughly chopped
1 small green pepper, seeded and finely sliced

Skin the chicken and cut the breasts into two; wash and pat dry on absorbent kitchen paper. Place 120ml/4 fl oz of the water in a liquidiser or food processor with the cashews, and blend to a smooth paste.

Melt the ghee or butter in a large pan over a medium heat and fry the ginger and garlic for 1 minute. Grind the spices in a mortar and pestle or coffee grinder. Reduce the heat, add the ground spices and fry for 1 minute. Increase the heat again, add the chicken and cook for 5-6 minutes, until the chicken changes colour. Add the cashew paste, and mix thoroughly. Rinse out the blender container with the remaining water and add it to the chicken with the salt. Mix well, cover the pan and cook over a low heat for 15 minutes, stirring occasionally. Add the carrots, cover and cook for a further 15 minutes, then add the peas and the sweetcorn, and cook, covered, over a medium heat for 5 minutes.

Reserve half the spring onions and add the rest to the chicken with the green pepper. Cook, uncovered, for 5-6 minutes, stirring frequently. Transfer the chicken to a serving dish and garnish with the reserved spring onions.

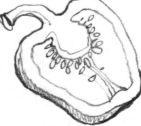

# CHICKEN KOHLAPURI

*The people of Kohlapur in southern India like very hot curries, flavoured with lots of chillies. The quantity of chillies is scaled down slightly in this recipe – increase it if you dare!*

Serves 4

### INGREDIENTS
4 large chicken breasts, skinned
1 large onion, roughly chopped
2-4 cloves garlic, peeled and
    roughly chopped
2.5cm/1 inch piece of fresh root
    ginger, peeled and roughly
    chopped
6 tbsps cooking oil
1 tsp ground turmeric
2 tsps ground coriander
1½ tsps ground cumin
1-1¼ tsps chilli powder

200g/7oz can of tomatoes
1¼ tsps salt
175ml/6 fl oz water
4-6 whole green chillies
1 tsp garam masala
2 tbsps freshly chopped
    coriander leaves

Cut each chicken breast into 2-3 pieces; wash and dry on absorbent kitchen paper. Place the onion, garlic and ginger in a liquidiser or food processor and blend to a smooth purée. Add a little water if necessary.

Heat the oil in a large pan over a medium heat and add the onion purée. Cook for 5-6 minutes, then add the turmeric, ground coriander, cumin and chilli powder; lower the heat and cook for 4-5 minutes stirring frequently. Add half the tomatoes, stir and cook for 2-3 minutes, then add the chicken and cook for 4-5 minutes, until chicken changes colour. Add the rest of the tomatoes, with all the juice from the can, the salt and water. Bring to the boil, cover and simmer until the chicken is tender, in about 20-30 minutes. Stir occasionally to ensure that the thickened sauce does not stick to the bottom of the pan. Add the whole green chillies and garam masala, and cook, covered, for a further 5 minutes. Remove the pan from the heat and stir in the coriander leaves. Season if necessary and serve.

# CHICKEN WITH CHANNA DHAL

*Channa dhal is only available in Indian supermarkets.*
*Yellow split peas are a suitable alternative and both go well*
*with chicken.*

Serves 6

### INGREDIENTS
225g/8oz channa dhal or yellow
  split peas
6 chicken joints

*Curry paste*
1 tbsp ground coriander
1 tsp ground turmeric
½ tsp cayenne or chilli powder
½ tsp freshly ground black
  pepper
1 tsp ground cinnamon
½ tsp ground nutmeg
60ml/2 fl oz water

2 tbsps cooking oil
2.5cm/1 inch piece of fresh root
  ginger, peeled and grated
3-4 cloves garlic, peeled and
  crushed
1 fresh green chilli, finely
  chopped
1¼ tsps salt
430ml/¾ pint warm water
45g/1½oz ghee or unsalted
  butter
1 large onion, finely sliced
2 tbsps freshly chopped
  coriander leaves
1 ripe tomato, sliced

Clean and wash the channa dhal
or the split peas and soak them
in plenty of cold water for about
2 hours. Drain well.

Cut each chicken joint into two,
separating legs from thighs. Wash
and pat dry on absorbent kitchen
paper. Blend the spices for the
curry paste with the water in a
small bowl. Heat the oil gently in
a heavy-based pan and fry the
ginger, garlic and green chilli for
1 minute. Add the spice paste,
and cook for 2-3 minutes then
add the chicken, increase the
heat slightly and cook the
chicken for 4-5 minutes, until it
changes colour. Add the dhal or
split peas, and cook for a further
3-4 minutes, then stir in the salt
and add the water. Bring to the
boil, cover the pan and simmer
until the chicken and the dhal
are tender – this will take about
35-40 minutes.

Meanwhile, in a separate pan,
melt the ghee or butter over a
medium heat and fry the onions
until they are golden brown,
stirring frequently. Add the
onions to the chicken along with
any remaining ghee in the pan.
Add half the coriander leaves
and stir until all the ingredients
are thoroughly mixed. Cover the
pan and simmer for 10 minutes.
Transfer the chicken to a serving
dish and garnish with the
tomatoes and remaining
coriander leaves.

# CHICKEN KORMA

*Chicken Korma is mild and creamy, an excellent curry to give to those who think that all Indian food is hot and spicy. I sometimes add a couple of tablespoons of poppy seeds for extra flavour and texture.*

Serves 4

### INGREDIENTS
4 chicken breasts, skin removed
2.5cm/1 inch piece of fresh root ginger, peeled and finely grated
150ml/¼ pint thick-set natural yogurt
1 small onion, roughly chopped
3-4 dried red chillies
2-4 cloves garlic, peeled and roughly chopped
5 tbsps cooking oil plus 2 tbsps extra oil
460g/1lb onions, finely sliced
1 tbsp ground coriander
½ tsp ground black pepper
1 tsp garam masala
1 tsp ground turmeric
150ml/¼ pint warm water
90g/3oz creamed coconut, cut into small pieces
1¼ tsps salt
2 tbsps ground almonds
Juice of ½ lemon

Cut each chicken breast into two, then mix with the ginger and yogurt, cover and leave to marinate in a cool place for 2-4 hours or in the refrigerator overnight.

Place the chopped onion, red chillies and garlic in a liquidiser or food processor and blend to a smooth paste. Add a little water if necessary. Heat the 5 tbsps of oil in a large pan over a medium heat and fry the sliced onions until they are golden brown. Remove the pan from the heat and, using a slotted spoon, transfer the onions to another dish. Leave any remaining oil in the pan. Add the remaining oil and return the pan to a medium heat. When hot, add the ground coriander, pepper, garam masala and turmeric, stir rapidly (take the pan off the heat if the oil is too hot) and add the chicken with the marinade. Cook for about 10 minutes, stirring frequently. Add the onion and chilli purée and continue to cook for 6-8 minutes on a low heat. Stir in the water and coconut and bring to the boil, stirring until the coconut is dissolved. Add the fried onion slices and salt. Reduce the heat to low, cover the pan and simmer until the chicken is tender about 25-30 minutes. Stir in the ground almonds, remove from the heat and add the lemon juice. Season if necessary and serve.

# CHICKEN DO-PIAZA

*Do-piaza literally means cooked with twice as much onion.
Be prepared to shed a tear or two whilst preparing this curry!
Some recipes suggest weighing the meat and then using
exactly twice as much onion – this recipe is less precise.*

Serves 4

## INGREDIENTS

4 large chicken breasts, skin removed
4 large onions, roughly chopped
2.5cm/1 inch piece of fresh root ginger, peeled and roughly chopped
3-4 cloves garlic, peeled and roughly chopped
4 tbsps cooking oil
1 tsp ground turmeric
1 tsp ground coriander
1 tsp ground cumin
¼-½ tsp chilli powder
200g/7oz can tomatoes
175ml/6 fl oz warm water
2 cinnamon sticks, each 5cm/2 inches long, broken up
4 green cardamoms, the top of each pod split open
4 whole cloves
2 dried bay leaves, crushed
1¼ tsp salt
2 level tbsps ghee or unsalted butter
1 large onion, finely sliced
1 tbsp freshly chopped coriander leaves

Cut each chicken breast into 3 pieces. Wash and dry on absorbent kitchen paper. Place the chopped onion, ginger and garlic in a liquidiser or food processor and blend to a smooth paste; add a little water, if necessary.

Heat the oil in a large pan over a medium heat and add the onion purée. Stir-fry for 4-5 minutes, then add the turmeric, coriander, cumin and chilli powder. Fry for 4-5 minutes stirring frequently. Add the juice from the canned tomatoes, a little at a time, to prevent the spices from sticking to the pan. Add the chicken and fry over a medium heat, until it has changed colour. Pour in the water with the cinnamon, cardamom, cloves, bay leaves, salt and the whole canned tomatoes. Bring to the boil, cover and simmer until the chicken is tender and the sauce is fairly thick – about 25 minutes. Cook uncovered, if necessary, for a little longer, to thicken the sauce.

Heat the ghee or butter and fry the sliced onion for 5 minutes. Add the onions and ghee to the chicken, stir in the coriander leaves, season and serve.

# CHICKEN WITH WHOLE SPICES

*This spicy chicken curry cooks quickly and does not require marinating. It is quite hot, especially if you get a whole chilli.*

Serves 6

## INGREDIENTS

6 chicken joints, skinned
4 tbsps cooking oil
1 tsp cumin seeds
1 large onion, finely chopped
1.25cm/½ inch piece of fresh root ginger, peeled and finely chopped
2-4 cloves garlic, peeled and crushed or finely chopped
2-3 dried whole red chillies
2 cinnamon sticks, 5cm/2 inches long, broken up
2 brown cardamoms, the top of each pod split open
4 whole cloves
10 whole allspice berries
½ tsp ground turmeric
1 tsp paprika
150ml/¼ pint warm water
1¼ tsps salt or to taste
2 ripe tomatoes, skinned and chopped
2 whole fresh green chillies
1 tbsp ground almonds
2 tbsps freshly chopped coriander leaves

Cut each chicken joint into two; separate legs from thighs and cut each breast in half. Heat the oil over a medium heat and fry the cumin seeds until they pop, then add the onion, ginger, garlic and red chillies. Fry until the onions are soft but not brown, stirring frequently. Add the cinnamon, cardamoms, cloves and allspice, and cook for a further 30 seconds. Stir in the turmeric and paprika and then the chicken. Stir fry over a medium heat for 5-6 minutes, until the chicken is white all over. Add the water and salt and bring to the boil, then cover the pan and simmer until the chicken is tender – about 30 minutes.

Add the tomatoes, green chillies and the ground almonds. Stir and mix well, then cover the pan again and simmer for a further 6-8 minutes. Stir in half the coriander leaves and remove the pan from heat. Transfer the chicken to a warmed serving dish and garnish with the remaining coriander.

# DAHI MURGHI

*Once the chicken has marinated in the yogurt, preferably overnight, this is quick to cook and requires little attention. Dahi Murghi is spicy yet creamy – just how I like my curries.*

Serves 6

### INGREDIENTS

6 chicken joints, skinned
150ml/¼ pint thick-set natural yogurt
3-4 cloves garlic, peeled and roughly chopped
2.5cm/1 inch piece of fresh root ginger, peeled and roughly chopped
2-3 dried red chillies
½ tsp ground turmeric
1 tbsp ground coriander
4 tbsps cooking oil
1 large onion, finely sliced
2-4 fresh green chillies, whole
1 tsp salt
½ tsp garam masala
2 tbsps freshly chopped coriander leaves

Cut each chicken joint into two, separate legs from thighs and cut each breast into two pieces. Wash the chicken and dry on absorbent kitchen paper. Place the yogurt, garlic, ginger, dried red chillies, turmeric and ground coriander in a liquidiser or food processor and blend until smooth. Arrange the chicken in a large dish and pour the marinade over. Mix thoroughly, cover and leave to marinate for 6-8 hours, or overnight in the refrigerator.

Place the chicken and marinade in a heavy-based frying pan with a lid over a medium heat. Stir-fry without the lid until the chicken is heated through. Cover the pan and simmer gently until the chicken is tender – about 25-30 minutes. Remove from the heat.

Heat the oil in a wide shallow pan over a medium heat, add the onions and cook until browned. Add the chicken and cook uncovered for 5-6 minutes, stirring frequently. Add the whole green chillies, salt and garam masala and cook for a further 3-4 minutes. Remove the pan from the heat and stir in half the coriander leaves. Put the chicken into a warmed serving dish and garnish with the remaining coriander leaves.

# CHICKEN TIKKA MASALA

*One of the best known chicken curries, this is moderately
spiced and served in a creamy almond sauce.*

Serves 4

### INGREDIENTS
460g/1lb Chicken Tikka (see
  recipe)
1.25cm/½ inch piece of fresh
  root ginger, peeled and
  roughly chopped
2 cloves garlic, peeled and
  roughly chopped
1 tsp salt
60g/2oz unsalted butter
1 small onion, finely chopped
¼ tsp ground turmeric
½ tsp ground cumin
½ tsp ground coriander
½ tsp garam masala
¼-½ tsp chilli powder
120ml/4 fl oz liquid, made up of
  the reserved juice from the
  Chicken Tikka and warm water
280ml/½ pint double cream
2 tbsps ground almonds

Prepare the chicken tikka as on
page 40. Mix together the
ginger, garlic and ½ a teaspoon
of salt and crush to a paste. Melt
the butter and fry the onions for
2-3 minutes. Add the ginger and
garlic paste and cook for 1
minute, then stir in the turmeric,
cumin, coriander, garam masala
and chilli powder. Cook for 2
minutes, stirring occasionally.
Add the liquid and stir gently,
then gradually add the cream,
and the remaining salt. Simmer
for 5 minutes and then add the
chicken. Lower the heat, cover
the pan and cook for 10 minutes.
Stir in the ground almonds and
simmer for a further 5-6 minutes,
before serving.

# MURGHI JHAL FREZI

*This is a richly spicy chicken curry, quite hot and very colourful. Serve with plain rice, Indian breads and a yogurt raita.*

Serves 6

## INGREDIENTS

6 chicken joints
3 large onions, finely chopped
175ml/6 fl oz water
2.5cm/1 inch piece of fresh root ginger, peeled and grated
2-4 cloves garlic, peeled and crushed
1 tsp ground coriander
1 tsp ground cumin
1 tsp ground ajwain or caraway
½ tsp ground turmeric
½ tsp chilli powder
2 cinnamon sticks, 5cm/2 inch long, broken up
2 brown cardamoms, the top of each pod split open
4 whole cloves
5 tbsps cooking oil
1¼ tsps salt
1 tbsp tomato purée
1-2 fresh green chillies, sliced lengthways; remove the seeds for a milder flavour
2 tbsps freshly chopped coriander leaves

Skin and cut each joint into two, separate the legs from thighs and cut each breast into two pieces. Wash the chicken and dry on absorbent kitchen paper. Place the chicken in a saucepan, add half the chopped onions, the water, ginger, garlic, coriander, cumin, ajwain, turmeric, chilli powder, cinnamon, cardamom and cloves. Bring to the boil, stir then cover and simmer for 20-25 minutes.

Heat the oil over a medium heat in a separate pan and fry the rest of the onions until they are golden brown. Add the chicken to the fried onions and continue cooking for about 5 minutes, until the chicken is browned. Add half the spiced liquid in which the chicken was cooked, and stir fry for 4-5 minutes until reduced. Add the rest of the liquid and fry for a further 4-5 minutes. Add salt, tomato purée, the green chillies and coriander leaves, stir and cook over a low heat for 5-6 minutes. Taste, season and serve.

84

# MURGHI AUR PALAK

*This is a classic chicken curry flavoured with spinach,
fennel, ground coriander and chillies – it is quite hot, so
serve with plain rice and a cooling cucumber raita.*

Serves 6

*INGREDIENTS*
6 chicken quarters, skinned
4 tbsps cooking oil
2 onions, finely chopped
2.5cm/1 inch piece of fresh root
  ginger, peeled and finely
  grated
2-3 cloves garlic, peeled and
  crushed

*Curry Paste*
1 tsp ground turmeric
1 tsp ground fennel
1 tsp ground coriander
½ tsp chilli powder
3 tbsps water

1½ tsps salt
90ml/3 fl oz warm water
1 tbsp ghee or unsalted butter
1-2 cloves garlic, peeled and
  finely chopped
6-8 curry leaves
½ tsp cumin seeds
½ tsp fennel seeds
1-2 dried red chillies, roughly
  chopped
460g/1lb fresh spinach *or*
  225g/8oz frozen leaf spinach,
  (defrosted and drained)
4 tbsps natural yogurt
½ tsp garam masala

Cut each chicken quarter in half,
separating legs from thighs and
cutting each breast lengthways
into two. Heat the oil over a
medium heat and fry the onions,
ginger and garlic until the onions
are lightly browned. Mix the
curry paste in a small bowl.
Lower the heat, add the spice
paste, and stir-fry for 4-5 minutes.
Rinse out the bowl with 2
tablespoons of water and add to
the spice mixture. Stir-fry for a
further 2-3 minutes. Add the
chicken and stir-fry over a
medium heat until the chicken
changes colour. Add 1 teaspoon
of salt and the water, bring to the
boil, then cover the pan and
simmer for 15 minutes; stir once
or twice during this time.

Melt the ghee or butter in a
separate pan over a medium heat
and add the garlic and curry
leaves followed by the cumin,
fennel and red chillies, then stir
briskly. Wash the fresh spinach
thoroughly, remove any hard
stalks and add the spinach and
the remaining salt. Stir-fry for 5-6
minutes. Mix the spinach and
chicken together in the larger
pan, bring to the boil, cover and
simmer for 20 minutes, stirring
occasionally.

Mix the yogurt and garam masala
together and beat until the yogurt
is smooth. Add to the chicken
and mix thoroughly. Cook,
uncovered, for 6-8 minutes over
medium heat, stirring frequently.
Taste, add extra salt if necessary,
and serve.

# CHICKEN DHANSAK

*A dhansak is a curry of meat or chicken cooked with lentils.
Sometimes, as in this recipe, two or more types of lentils or
dried peas are used. Dhansak seasoning is usually of
medium heat. Tamarind concentrate is available from
Indian grocers.*

Serves 6

### INGREDIENTS
6 chicken portions, skinned
1 tsp salt
2.5cm/1 inch piece of fresh root
  ginger, peeled and roughly
  chopped
4-6 cloves garlic, peeled and
  chopped

### Mixed Spices
1 tsp coriander seeds
1 tsp cumin seeds
1 tsp fennel seeds
4 green cardamoms
1 cinnamon stick, 5cm/2 inches
  long, broken up
4-6 dried red chillies
10 black peppercorns
2 bay leaves
¼ tsp fenugreek seeds
½ tsp black mustard seeds

2 tbsps ghee or unsalted butter
120ml/4 fl oz warm water

### For the Dhal
90g/3oz toor dhal (yellow split
  peas)
90g/3oz masoor dhal (red lentils)
5 tbsps cooking oil
1 large onion, finely chopped
1 tsp ground turmeric
1 tsp garam masala
570ml/1 pint warm water
1 tsp salt
1 tsp tamarind concentrate *or* 1½
  tbsps lemon juice
1 tbsp freshly chopped coriander
  leaves

Wash and dry the chicken portions and cut each portion into two. Add the salt to the ginger and garlic and crush to a pulp. Grind the spices together, then make into a paste with the ginger and garlic pulp and 6 tablespoons of water. Coat the chicken in the marinade and leave for 4-6 hours, or overnight in the refrigerator.

Melt the ghee or butter in a large frying pan over a medium heat and fry the chicken for 6-8 minutes, stirring frequently. Add the water, bring to the boil, cover and simmer for 20 minutes. Stir several times.

Meanwhile, mix together the toor and masoor dhals, wash and drain well. Heat the oil over a medium heat and fry the onions for 5 minutes, stirring frequently. Add the turmeric and garam masala, and continue cooking for 1 minute. Add the dhal, lower the heat and fry for 5 minutes, stirring frequently. Add the water

and salt, bring to the boil, cover and simmer the dhal for 30 minutes until soft, stirring occasionally. Press the dhal through a sieve using a metal spoon, discard the fibrous mixture left in the sieve. Pour the sieved dhal over the chicken, cover and bring to the boil, then reduce the heat and simmer for 20-25 minutes. Stir occasionally during the first half of the cooking time, but more frequently during the latter half, to ensure that the mixture does not stick to the bottom of the pan.

Dissolve the tamarind pulp in 3 tablespoons of boiling water. Add this to the chicken, stir and mix thoroughly. Cover and simmer for 5 minutes. Stir in the coriander leaves and serve. If using lemon juice, simply add this at the end of the cooking time, once the chicken is cooked through and tender.

# DUM KA MURGHI

*A simple, delicious way of cooking chicken which is suitable for joints or a whole bird. Chicken pieces will, of course, cook more quickly.*

Serves 4

*INGREDIENTS*
1 onion, finely minced
2 tsps ground coriander
1 tsp chilli powder
¼ tsp turmeric powder
1 tbsp tomato purée
1 tsp fresh root ginger, peeled and grated
2-3 cloves garlic, peeled and crushed
½ tsp salt
150ml/¼ pint natural yogurt
1.4kg/3lb chicken, cut into 8 joints
Oil

Preheat the oven to 190°C/375°F/Gas Mark 5. Mix the onion, coriander, chilli, turmeric, tomato, ginger, garlic and salt with the yogurt. Rub the mixture all over the chicken pieces, then brush them with oil. Bake in the preheated oven for 50 to 60 minutes, brushing with oil frequently, until the liquid has evaporated and the chicken is cooked.

To cook a whole chicken in this way, bake with the spices wrapped in baking foil for 1½ to 1¾ hours, then evaporate the liquid.

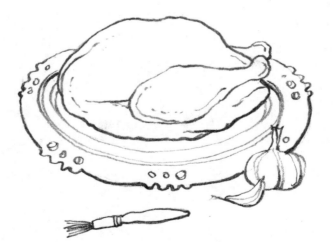

# MALABARI CHICKEN

*This is a rich, fruity chicken curry, delicious with pilau rice
or naan breads.*

Serves 4-6

### INGREDIENTS
1 large onion, chopped
60g/2oz ghee or 3 tbsps oil
2.5cm/1 inch cinnamon stick
6 green cardamoms
6 cloves
1 bay leaf
1 tsp fresh root ginger, peeled
   and grated
2-3 cloves garlic, peeled and
   crushed
1.4kg/3lb chicken, cut into 8
   pieces
1 tsp chilli powder
1 tsp ground cumin
1 tsp ground coriander
150ml/¼ pint natural yogurt
1 tsp salt
15g/½oz creamed coconut
15g/½oz blanched almonds,
   sliced
15g/½oz raisins
120ml/4 fl oz water
2 tbsps evaporated milk
1 tbsp freshly chopped coriander
   leaves
2 green chillies, chopped
   (optional)
225g/8oz pineapple, cut into
   chunks, fresh or canned

Fry the onion in the ghee or oil
until soft, then add the
cinnamon, cardamoms, cloves,
bay leaf and fry for 1 minute.
Add the ginger and garlic and
stir-fry for 30 seconds, then add
the chicken. Stir and cook for 2-3
minutes. Add the chilli, cumin
and coriander, stir well and add
the yogurt and salt. Cover and
cook for 10 minutes or until the
yogurt is dry and the oil
separates. Add the creamed
coconut, almonds, raisins and
water, cover and cook for 20-30
minutes.

Add the evaporated milk and
cook for 5 minutes, then stir in
the coriander, green chillies and
pineapple chunks. Cook for a
further 5 minutes.

# CHICKEN TOMATO

*Without the spices this dish could be from almost anywhere in the world. With the spices it is deliciously Indian!*

Serves 4

### INGREDIENTS
1 onion, chopped
3 tbsps oil *or* 40g/1½oz ghee
2.5cm/1 inch cinnamon stick
1 bay leaf
6 cloves
6 green cardamoms
2.5cm/1 inch fresh root ginger, peeled and sliced
4 cloves garlic, peeled and chopped
1.4kg/3lb roasting chicken, jointed into 8 pieces
1 tsp chilli powder
1 tsp ground cumin
1 tsp ground coriander
400g/14oz can tomatoes, crushed
1 tsp salt
1 tbsp freshly chopped coriander
2 green chillies, halved

Fry the onion for 2 minutes in the oil or ghee. Add the cinnamon, bay leaf, cloves, cardamoms and fry for 1 minute, then add the ginger and garlic and cook for a further 30 seconds. Add the chicken pieces, sprinkle them with chilli powder, cumin and coriander and fry for 2-3 minutes, then add the crushed tomatoes. Season with salt and add the coriander and chillies. Mix well, cover and cook for 40-45 minutes until the chicken is tender.

# MEAT

Although a large number of Indians are vegetarian there are many who do eat meat, and the classic Indian cuisine contains a vast selection of recipes for meat dishes. Beef and pork are far less common than mutton and lamb and a very traditional meat is goat. Many classic meat dishes were developed for goat but are now made with lamb outside India as it is more tender and far more palatable. I can think of no other red meat which absorbs the flavours of spices as readily as lamb and roasted, curried or as kababs, it is my favourite meat for Indian and all other meat cookery. Mutton, which is virtually unobtainable in the UK, is the most common meat eaten in India but, despite this fact, most of the recipes which follow in this chapter have been adapted for lamb.

## Pork, a West Coast Speciality

Pork is mainly eaten on the west coast of India, in the Christian communities around Goa. It blends well with coconut and there is an excellent recipe here for Goan Curry which makes a very pleasant change from the more common dishes of mutton and beef. Many of the meat-eating Hindus would be quite happy to eat pork but they simply don't get the opportunity to do so as pigs are only raised in a relatively small area. The Moslems, however, would not eat pork as it is considered to be unclean.

## Mutton and Lamb – Meat for All

The vast majority of the Indian population are Hindu and those people who do eat meat would not eat any flesh from the cow, which is considered to be sacred. With the Moslem ban on pork and the Hindus not eating beef or veal, it is safest to cook with mutton or goat in order to avoid giving offence in India, and to keep lamb for special occasions and feasts.

## Not all Meat Dishes are Curries

We tend to label all Indian dishes as curries but this is about as true as saying that every English meat dish is a roast! It is simply a convenient label which we all wrongly apply. Now, having said that, I have been unable to track down an authoritative definition of a curry and must deduce that it is a mix of spices, fried and cooked with other ingredients to a sauce which may then be used to cook meat, chicken, vegetables, fish or pulses. Thus dishes that are dry cooked, grilled, baked or roasted are not curries and should not be referred to as such.

There are a few terms commonly used in Indian meat cookery that you will very quickly learn and which will help you to identify the type of dish that they describe. For example, *koftas* are meatballs and *keema* is the word for mince, so all keema dishes will contain minced meat, usually mutton but beef or lamb may be used.

## A Kebab by any other Name

As with all cuisines founded on a pot pouri of dishes collected from many regions there are often a number of similar words used to describe the same basic dish. The word that confuses me most in Indian cooking is *kabab*, which I have always thought to be *kebab*. However, I have adopted the former spelling throughout this book. Kababs are usually pieces of meat threaded onto skewers for cooking, but occasionally kababs are made from baked meats that are then served on cocktail sticks as nibbles or cocktail party foods.

## Marinating for Tenderness and the Perfect Flavour

Many Indian dishes call for the meat to be marinated, either in a fairly dry mix of lightly roasted spices, or in a yogurt sauce flavoured with spices. This custom stems back to times when the meat required this treatment to make it edible – neither goat nor mutton are renowned for their tenderness! With the better cuts of meat this custom is continued more for the benefit of the flavour of the finished dish than for the texture of the meat.

Meat that has been diced should be evenly coated in the marinade. Larger pieces and whole joints benefit from being pierced at regular intervals with a small, sharp knife, allowing the marinade to penetrate right to the bone and thus to flavour all the meat and not just the surface. Meat that has been marinated cooks slightly more quickly, and cooking times should be adjusted accordingly, especially when roasting.

# MEAT DILPASAND

*I love using poppy seeds in curries – they add a slightly nutty flavour and texture to the dish. I scatter a handful of poppy seeds over this curry for garnish before serving.*

Serves 4-6

### INGREDIENTS
1kg/2¼lb leg of lamb
150g/5oz thick-set natural yogurt
1 tsp ground turmeric
2 tbsps white poppy seeds
2.5cm/1 inch piece of fresh root ginger, peeled and roughly chopped
4-5 cloves garlic, peeled and roughly chopped
1-2 fresh green chillies, seeded if a milder flavour is preferred
460g/1lb onions
40g/1½oz ghee or unsalted butter
½ tsp chilli powder
1 tsp paprika
1 tbsp ground cumin
1 tsp garam masala
1 tbsp tomato purée
1¼ tsps salt
175ml/6 fl oz warm water
30g/1oz creamed coconut *or* 2 tbsps desiccated coconut
2 tbsps freshly chopped coriander leaves

Trim any surplus fat from the meat, and cut the meat into 4cm/1½ inch cubes. Add the yogurt and turmeric, mix thoroughly, cover and leave to marinate for 4-6 hours or overnight in the refrigerator.

Roast the poppy seeds without fat over a gentle heat until they are a little darker – allow to cool. Place the ginger, garlic and green chillies in a blender or food processor. Chop one onion and add it to the ginger and garlic mixture. Blend until fairly smooth. Chop the remaining onions finely.

Melt the ghee or butter over a medium heat and fry the onions until golden brown. Reduce the heat and add the chilli powder, paprika, cumin and ½ tsp garam masala. Stir and fry for 2-3 minutes, then add the liquidised ingredients and cook for 10-12 minutes, stirring frequently. If during this time the spices tend to stick to the bottom of the pan, add 1 tbsp of water at a time as and when necessary. Add the meat and fry for 4-5 minutes over a medium heat, stirring constantly. Stir in the tomato purée, salt and water, bring to the boil, cover and simmer for 45 minutes or until the meat is tender. Stir occasionally during the first half of cooking, but more frequently towards the end, to ensure that the thickened gravy does not stick to the bottom of the pan.

If you are using creamed coconut, cut it into small pieces with a sharp knife. Desiccated coconut should be ground in a coffee grinder or pestle and mortar before use to ensure that the necessary fine texture is achieved in making the curry. Grind the poppy seeds and stir into the meat with the coconut. Stir until the coconut is dissolved. Cover and simmer for 15 minutes. Stir in the coriander leaves and the remaining garam masala, then serve immediately.

# MEAT MADRAS

*Madras is the major city of southern India and has given its name to the hot spicy style of curry popular throughout the south.*

Serves 4-6

### INGREDIENTS
6 tbsps cooking oil
2 onions, roughly chopped
2.5cm/1 inch piece of fresh root ginger, peeled and roughly chopped
3-4 cloves garlic, peeled and roughly chopped
4-6 dried red chillies
2 large cloves garlic, peeled and crushed
1-2 fresh green chillies, sliced lengthways
200g/7oz can tomatoes
3 tsps ground cumin
1 tsp ground coriander
½-1 tsp chilli powder
1 tsp ground turmeric
1kg/2¼lb leg or shoulder of lamb, trimmed and cut into 4cm/1½ inch cubes
175ml/6 fl oz warm water
1¼ tsps salt
1 tsp garam masala

Heat 3 tbsps of oil over a medium heat and fry the onions, ginger, chopped garlic and red chillies until the onions are soft, stirring frequently. Remove from the heat and allow to cool.

Meanwhile, heat the remaining oil over a medium heat and fry the crushed garlic and green chillies until the garlic is lightly browned. Add half the tomatoes, with the juice; stir and cook for 1-2 minutes, then add the cumin, coriander, chilli powder and turmeric. Reduce the heat to low and cook for 6-8 minutes, stirring frequently. Add the meat and raise the heat to medium-high. Stir and fry for about 5 minutes, until the meat changes colour. Add the water, bring to the boil, cover and simmer for 30 minutes.

Blend the fried onions in a blender or food processor with the remaining tomatoes until smooth. Add to the meat – bring to the boil, add the salt and mix well. Cover the pan and simmer for a further 35-40 minutes or until the meat is tender. Stir in the garam masala and serve.

# LAMB WITH MUNG BEANS

*This curry really takes three days to cook – the mung beans*
*require soaking on day one, the curry is cooked on day two*
*and left to cool then it is actually eaten on day three, by*
*which time all the flavours have blended perfectly.*

Serves 6-8

## INGREDIENTS

150g/6oz whole mung beans,
  soaked overnight
1¼ tsps salt
2.5cm/1 inch piece of fresh root
  ginger, peeled and roughly
  chopped
2-4 cloves garlic, peeled and
  roughly chopped
680g/1½lbs boneless leg or
  shoulder of lamb, cut into
  2.cm/1 inch cubes
420ml/¾ pint water
1 large onion, finely chopped

*Spices*
2 dried red chillies
1½ tsps cumin seeds
2 tsps coriander seeds
4 whole cloves
1 cinnamon stick, 5cm/2 inches
  long, broken up
4 black peppercorns

1 tsp ground turmeric
200g/7oz can tomatoes, *or* 4 ripe
  tomatoes, skinned and
  chopped
2 tbsps freshly chopped
  coriander leaves

Soak the mung beans overnight
in plenty of cold water, then
drain well. Pulses usually contain
a certain amount of grit and
sand; make sure you clean the
beans and wash them several
times before soaking.

Add the salt to the ginger and
garlic and crush them to a
smooth pulp. Place the meat and
water in a large pan and bring to
the boil. Cover the pan and
simmer for 45 minutes. Add the
mung beans with the chopped
onion. Return to the boil, cover
the pan and simmer for a further
25 minutes. Add the ginger and
garlic pulp. Grind the spices and
add them with the turmeric and
the tomatoes. Simmer for 10
minutes, uncovered.

Remove the pan from the heat
and leave it for several hours
before serving. The longer you
let it stand, the better – overnight
is ideal. Reheat the curry, stir in
the coriander leaves and simmer
for 5 minutes before serving.

# MEAT DURBARI

*Classic Indian dishes used for banquets and other great occasions tend to be quite luxurious! 'Durbar' means a formal gathering, so this is a lamb dish served on such occasions.*

Serves 4

*INGREDIENTS*
1kg/2¼lb leg of lamb

*Curry Paste:*
1 tbsp mustard seeds
1 tbsp sesame seeds
2 tbsps white poppy seeds
10 black peppercorns
2-4 dried red chillies
1 bay leaf, crushed
5cm/2 inch piece of cinnamon
  stick, broken up
4 whole cloves
Inner seeds of 2 brown
  cardamoms
3 tbsps white wine vinegar

1¼ tsps salt
3-4 cloves garlic, peeled and
  roughly chopped
40g/1½oz ghee or unsalted
  butter
1 large onion, finely chopped
2.5cm/1 inch piece of fresh root
  ginger, peeled and finely
  grated
175ml/6 fl oz warm water
1 tbsp tomato purée
2 fresh green chillies, slit
  lengthways into halves, seeded
  for a milder flavour
2 tbsps freshly chopped
  coriander leaves

Trim any excess fat from the meat, and cut the meat into 5cm/2 inch cubes. Grind the spices for the curry paste in a grinder or pestle and mortar, then add the vinegar. Rub the spice paste into the meat and leave to marinate for 4-6 hours, or overnight in the refrigerator.

Add the salt to the garlic and crush to a smooth pulp. Melt the ghee or butter gently over a low heat, add the onions and ginger and fry until the onions are soft: Add the garlic paste and fry for a further 2-3 minutes, stirring frequently, then add the meat and cook until all sides of the meat are sealed and brown. Add the water, bring to the boil, then cover and simmer until the meat is tender – about 30-40 minutes. Add the tomato purée, green chillies and coriander leaves – increase the heat to medium and cook for 3-4 minutes, stirring continuously. Remove the pan from the heat, season to taste and serve.

# PASANDA BADAM CURRY

*A pasanda is a curry from the north of India, rich, creamy
and amongst my favourites!*

Serves 4-6

### INGREDIENTS
900g/2lbs boneless leg of lamb
2.5cm/1 inch piece of fresh root
   ginger, peeled and roughly
   chopped
4-6 cloves garlic, peeled and
   roughly chopped
2 fresh green chillies, seeded and
   roughly chopped
4 tbsps natural yogurt
60g/2oz ghee or unsalted butter
3 onions, finely sliced
½ tsp ground turmeric
1 tsp ground cumin
2 tsps ground coriander
½ tsp ground nutmeg
¼-½ tsp chilli powder
225ml/8 fl oz warm water
1¼ tsps salt
150ml/¼ pint single cream
30g/1oz ground almonds
1 tsp garam masala or ground
   mixed spice
2 tbsps rose-water
½ tsp paprika

·Beat the lamb with a steak mallet
to a thickness of 6mm/¼ inch,
then cut it into thin slices, about
4cm/1½ inches long and
1.25cm½ inch wide. Place the
ginger, garlic, green chillies and
yogurt in a liquidiser or food
processor and blend until
smooth. Melt the ghee or butter
over a medium heat and fry the
onions until they are lightly
browned. Add the turmeric,
cumin, coriander, nutmeg and
chilli powder; reduce the heat
and cook for 2-3 minutes. Stir in
the meat and fry it over a high
heat for 3-4 minutes or until it
changes colour, then add about 2
tbsps of the yogurt mixture and
cook for 1-2 minutes, stirring
frequently. Repeat this process
until all the yogurt mixture is
used up.

Fry the meat over a medium heat
for 4-5 minutes, stirring
frequently. When the fat begins
to seep through the thick spice
paste and floats on the surface,
add the water. Bring to the boil,
cover the pan and simmer until
the meat is tender for about 1
hour, stirring occasionally.

Add the salt, cream and ground
almonds to the pasanda and let it
simmer uncovered for 5-6
minutes. Stir in the garam masala
and rose-water and remove from
the heat. Transfer the pasanda to
a warmed serving dish and
sprinkle the paprika on top.

# BHOONA GOSHT

*To cook this dish really well it is important to fry each ingredient over the correct heat. 'Bhoona Gosht' literally means fried meat.*

Serves 4-6

## INGREDIENTS

1kg/2¼lbs boneless leg or shoulder of lamb
5 tbsps cooking oil
3 large onions, finely chopped
2.5cm/1 inch piece of fresh root ginger, peeled and grated or finely chopped
3-4 cloves garlic, peeled and crushed
1 tsp ground turmeric
2 tsps ground cumin
1 tbsp ground coriander
½-1 tsp chilli powder
200ml/7 fl oz warm water
1¼ tsps salt
2 ripe tomatoes, skinned and chopped; canned tomatoes may be used
4-5 whole fresh green chillies
1 tsp garam masala
1 tbsp freshly chopped coriander leaves
2 small ripe tomatoes, sliced

Trim off any excess fat from the meat, then cut the meat into 2.5cm/1 inch cubes. Heat the oil over a medium heat and add the onions, ginger and garlic. Fry until the onions are just soft, then lower the heat and add the turmeric, cumin, coriander and chilli powder. Stir and fry for 2-3 minutes. Add the meat, increase the heat to medium and fry for 5 minutes, stirring frequently.

Cover the pan and cook on the medium heat until all the liquid has disappeared for about 15-20 minutes. Stir frequently.

Turn the heat to high and fry the meat for 2-3 minutes stirring continuously. Reduce the heat again to medium and fry for a further 7-8 minutes, stirring frequently. The meat should now look fairly dry and the fat should have separated out. Some of the fat can be drained off at this stage, but be careful not to drain off any of the spices. Add the water and salt, bring to the boil, cover and simmer for 50-60 minutes or until the meat is tender. Add more water if necessary. At the end of the cooking time, the thick spice paste should be clinging to the pieces of meat.

Add the chopped tomatoes and the whole green chillies. Cook for 3-4 minutes, then stir in the garam masala and half the coriander leaves. Turn the bhoona gosht into a warmed serving dish and arrange the sliced tomatoes over the meat. Scatter the remaining coriander leaves over the curry before serving.

# SHAHI (ROYAL) KORMA

*Kormas are always rich, mild and creamy but this one is
extra special. 'Shahi' means royal, so this is a royal dish,
perfect for a dinner party.*

Serves 4-6

*INGREDIENTS*

1kg/2¼lbs boneless leg of lamb,
  trimmed and cut into 4cm/1½
  inch cubes
150g/5oz thick-set natural yogurt
1.25cm/½ inch piece of fresh
  root ginger, peeled and grated
3-4 cloves of garlic, peeled and
  crushed
60g/2oz ghee or unsalted butter
2 onions, finely chopped

2 tbsps coriander seeds
8 green cardamoms
10 whole black peppercorns
3-4 dried red chillies

1 tsp ground cinnamon
1 tsp ground mace

3-4 tbsps freshly chopped fresh
  mint, *or* 1½ tsps dried or
  bottled mint
60g/2oz ground almonds
280ml/½ pint warm water
½ tsp saffron strands, crushed
1½ tsps salt
60g/2oz raw split cashews
150ml/¼ pint single cream
1 tbsp rose-water

Place the meat into a bowl with
the yogurt, ginger and garlic. Mix
thoroughly, cover the bowl and
leave to marinate for 2-4 hours or
overnight in the refrigerator.

Place the marinated meat, with
any remaining marinade in a
heavy-based saucepan over a
medium-low heat. Bring to a
slow simmer, then cover and
cook the meat in its own juice
for 45-50 minutes, stirring
occasionally. Take the pan off
the heat and remove the meat
with a slotted spoon. Transfer the
meat to a dish and keep hot.

Grind the whole spices then add
the cinnamon and mace. Melt the
ghee over a medium heat and fry
the onions until they are lightly
browned, then reduce the heat to
low and add the ground spices
and the mint; stir and fry for 2-3
minutes. Add half of the liquid
from the meat, stir and cook for
1-2 minutes. Add the ground
almonds and mix thoroughly;
then add the remaining liquid
from the meat, stir and cook for
a further 1-2 minutes. Increase
the heat to medium and add the
meat, stir and cook the meat for
5-6 minutes. Add the water,
saffron strands, salt and cashews,
bring to a slow boil, then cover
and simmer for 20 minutes. Add
the cream, stir and mix well,
simmer very slowly uncovered
for 6-8 minutes, then stir in the
rose-water and remove from the
heat.

# ALOO GOSHT

*This potato and lamb curry can be made even more special
by the use of sweet potatoes, giving a richly rounded flavour.*

Serves 4-6

*INGREDIENTS*
1kg/2¼lb leg or shoulder of lamb
1¼ tsps salt
2.5cm/1 inch piece of fresh root
  ginger, peeled and roughly
  chopped
3-4 cloves garlic, peeled and
  roughly chopped
30g/1oz ghee or unsalted butter
460g/1lb potatoes, peeled and
  cut into 4cm/1½ inch cubes
3 tbsps cooking oil
1 large onion, finely chopped
3-4 dried red chillies
2 cinnamon sticks, 5cm/2-inch
  long, broken up

*Spice Paste*
1 tbsp ground coriander
1 tsp ground allspice
1 tsp paprika
1 tsp ground turmeric
¼-½ tsp chilli powder
3 tbsps water

1 tbsp tomato purée
2 brown cardamoms, top of each
  pod split open
4-6 whole cloves
430ml/¾ pint warm water
1 tbsp lemon juice
2 tbsps freshly chopped
  coriander leaves

Trim any excess fat from the meat and cut the meat into 4cm/1½ inch cubes. Add the salt to the ginger and garlic and crush to a pulp. Melt the ghee or butter over a medium heat in a non-stick or cast iron pan and fry the potatoes until they are well-browned on all sides, in about 10 minutes. Remove the potatoes with a slotted spoon and keep to one side. Add the oil to any remaining ghee in the pan and, when hot, fry the onions, red chillies and cinnamon sticks until the onions are soft. Add the ginger and garlic pulp, and fry for a further 2-3 minutes stirring frequently. Reduce the heat to low and add the spice paste, stir and fry for 3-4 minutes, then add the meat. Increase the heat to medium-high and fry for 5-6 minutes until the meat changes colour, then stir in the tomato purée. Add the cardamoms, cloves and water. Bring to the boil, cover and simmer for 45-50 minutes.

Add the fried potatoes, bring to the boil again, cover and simmer for 15-20 minutes or until the potatoes are tender. Remove from the heat and add the lemon juice and coriander leaves before serving.

# MEAT VINDALOO

*Vindaloo is a hot curry (too hot for me!) and the heat is accentuated by the use of vinegar in the marinade. Adjust the number of chillies if you wish.*

Serves 4-6

### INGREDIENTS
*Whole Spices*
2 tbsps coriander seeds
1 tbsp cumin seeds
6-8 dried red chillies
1 tbsp mustard seeds
½ tsp fenugreek seeds

3-4 tbsps cider or white wine vinegar
1 tsp ground turmeric
2.5cm/1 inch piece of fresh root ginger, peeled and finely grated
3-4 cloves garlic, peeled and crushed
1kg/2¼lbs boneless shoulder of lamb or stewing steak
4 tbsps cooking oil
1 large onion, finely chopped
1-2 tsps chilli powder
1 tsp paprika
1¼ tsps salt
430ml/¾ pint warm water
2-3 potatoes
1 tbsp freshly chopped coriander leaves (optional)

Grind the whole spices together then add the vinegar to make a paste. Add the turmeric, ginger and garlic, and mix thoroughly. Trim any excess fat from the meat then cut the meat into 2.5cm/1 inch cubes. Add the meat to the spices and mix well so that all the pieces are fully coated with the paste. Cover and leave to marinate for 4-6 hours or overnight in the refrigerator.

Place the meat in a pan over a medium heat, and cook for 5 minutes. Cover the pan, and cook the meat in its own juice for 15-20 minutes, or until the liquid is reduced to a thick paste. Stir occasionally during this time to ensure that the meat does not stick to the bottom of the pan. Remove from the heat and set to one side.

Heat the oil in a large pan over a medium heat and fry the onions until they are soft, then add the meat and fry for 6-8 minutes stirring frequently. Add the chilli powder, paprika and salt, stir and fry for a further 2-3 minutes, then add the water. Bring to the boil, cover and simmer for 40-45 minutes or until the meat is nearly tender (beef will take longer to cook, and you may need to add more water, during cooking).

Meanwhile, peel and wash the potatoes. Cut them into approximately 4cm/1½ inch cubes. Add to the meat and bring to the boil again. Cover the pan and simmer until the potatoes are cooked in 15-20 minutes. Turn the vindaloo onto a warmed serving dish and garnish with the coriander leaves.

# NAWABI KHEEMA PILAU (MINCED LAMB PILAU)

*This mouthwatering pilau is unusual as it includes minced lamb in the rice. Serve with a vegetable curry of your choice.*

Serves 4-6

### INGREDIENTS

275g/10oz basmati rice
1 tbsp ghee or unsalted butter
30g/1oz sultanas
30g/1oz raw cashews, split into halves
2 tbsps milk
1 tsp saffron strands
60g/2oz ghee or unsalted butter
6 green cardamoms, the top of each pod split open
4 whole cloves
1 tsp cumin seeds
2 bay leaves, crushed
2.5cm/1 inch piece of fresh root ginger, peeled and grated
2-3 cloves garlic, peeled and crushed
1-2 fresh green chillies, finely chopped, seeded if a milder flavour is preferred
1 tsp ground nutmeg
1 tsp ground cinnamon
1 tsp ground cumin
1 tbsp ground coriander
460g/1lb lean minced lamb
570ml/1 pint water
1¼ tsps salt
150ml/¼ pint single cream
2 tbsps rose-water
2 hard-boiled eggs, sliced

Wash and soak the basmati rice in cold water for 30 minutes, then drain. Melt the 1 tbsp of ghee or butter over a low heat and fry the sultanas until they swell, then remove them with a slotted spoon and set to one side. Fry the cashews in the same fat until they are lightly browned, then remove them with a slotted spoon and set to one side.

Boil the milk, add the saffron strands and leave until required. Melt the remaining 60g/2oz of ghee or butter gently over a low heat and fry the cardamoms, cloves, cumin seeds and bay leaves for 1 minute. Add the ginger, garlic and green chillies and stir fry for 30 seconds, then add the nutmeg, ground cinnamon, cumin and coriander and fry for 1 minute. Stir in the mince and increase the heat to medium. Stir-fry the mince until all the liquid dries up and it is lightly browned. This will take about 5 minutes. Add the rice, stir and fry for a further 5 minutes, then add the water, salt, cream and the steeped saffron and milk. Stir and mix well. Bring the liquid to the boil, cover the pan and simmer for 12-15 minutes without lifting the lid. Remove the pan from the heat and leave it undisturbed for a further 10-15 minutes.

Add half the nuts and raisins to the rice, then sprinkle the rose-water evenly over the top. Using a fork, mix them gently into the rice. Turn the pilau into a warmed serving dish and garnish with the remaining nuts and raisins and the sliced hard-boiled eggs.

# MEAT DILRUBA

*This delicious meat curry is in a class of its own. It is cooked
in two stages making it easier to get much of the preparation
and cooking out of the way in advance.*

Serves 4-6

## INGREDIENTS

1kg/2¼lbs boneless leg of lamb
1¼ tsps salt
1.25cm/½ inch piece of fresh
  root ginger, peeled and finely
  chopped
3-4 cloves garlic, peeled and
  finely chopped
1 tsp ground turmeric
150g/5oz thick-set natural yogurt
1 large onion, finely sliced
3-4 dried red chillies, roughly
  chopped
150ml/¼ pint water

1 tbsp white poppy seeds
1 tsp fenugreek seeds

60g/2oz desiccated coconut

2 tbsps ghee or unsalted butter
2 tbsps ground coriander
150ml/¼ pint milk
4-5 tbsps freshly chopped
  coriander leaves
1 fresh green chilli, cut
  lengthways into thin strips,
  seeds removed if preferred

Trim any excess fat from the
meat, then cut the meat into
2.5cm/1 inch cubes. Place the
ginger, garlic and salt in a pestle
and mortar and crush them to a
pulp. Alternatively, use a
chopping board and crush them
with the end of a wooden rolling
pin. Mix together the ginger and
garlic pulp, the turmeric and the
yogurt and beat until the mixture
is smooth. Add this to the meat,
mix thoroughly, cover and leave
to marinate for 4-6 hours or
overnight in the refrigerator.

Place the marinated meat in a
heavy-based saucepan, add the
onion, red chillies and the water.
Bring to a slow simmer over a
gentle heat. Cover the pan and
simmer for 50-60 minutes or until
the meat is tender. Remove from
the heat.

Grind the poppy and fenugreek
seeds, then grind the desiccated
coconut separately. Melt the ghee
over a medium heat and add the
ground coriander, stir and fry for
30 seconds. Add the ground
poppy and fenugreek seeds and
fry until the mixture is lightly
browned, stirring constantly.
Remove the meat from the
cooking liquor and add it to the
poppy and fenugreek mixture.
Stir and fry over a medium-high
heat until all the moisture
evaporates in 6-7 minutes. Add
the ground coconut, and fry for 2
minutes, then add the milk and
the liquid in which the meat was
cooked. Stir and mix thoroughly.
Cook, uncovered, over a low
heat for 4-5 minutes, stirring
frequently. Stir in the coriander
leaves and the green chilli,
remove from the heat and serve.

# MEAT MAHARAJA

*A rich lamb curry with poppy seeds and ground almonds –
fit for the Maharajas.*

Serves 4-6

## INGREDIENTS

4 tbsps ghee or unsalted butter
2 large onions, roughly chopped
2.5cm/1 inch piece of fresh root
 ginger, peeled and roughly
 chopped
4-6 cloves garlic, peeled and
 roughly chopped
1 fresh green chilli, seeded and
 chopped
1-2 dried red chillies, chopped
150g/5oz thick-set natural yogurt
1 tsp black cumin seeds or
 caraway seeds
3 tsps ground coriander
1 tsp garam masala
1 tsp ground turmeric
¼ tsp ground black pepper
2 tbsps white poppy seeds,
 ground
1kg/2¼lbs boneless leg of lamb,
 cut into 2.5cm/1 inch cubes
1¼ tsps salt
2 tbsps ground almonds
2 tbsps freshly chopped
 coriander leaves
1 tbsp lemon juice
30g/1oz unsalted pistachio nuts,
 lightly crushed

Melt 2 tbsps of the ghee over a
medium heat and fry the onions,
ginger, garlic, green and red
chillies until the onions are just
soft. Remove from the heat and
allow to cool slightly. Place the
yogurt in a liquidiser or food
processor, add the onion mixture
and blend to a purée. Set to one
side.

Heat the remaining ghee or
butter over a low heat (do not
overheat the ghee) and add the
black cumin or caraway seeds.
Mix the ground spices together
and add them with the ground
poppy seeds. Stir and fry for 1
minute, then add the meat,
increase the heat to medium-
high, stir and fry for 4-5 minutes
until the meat changes colour.
Cover the pan and let the meat
cook in its own juices for 15
minutes. Stir occasionally.

Add the yogurt and onion purée
and mix thoroughly. Rinse out
the liquidiser container with
175ml/6 fl oz warm water and
add this to the meat. Stir in the
salt and bring to the boil, cover
the pan and simmer until the
meat is tender, about 40 minutes.
Stir occasionally during the first
half of the cooking time, but
more frequently towards the end
to ensure that the thickened
sauce does not stick to the
bottom of the pan. Stir in the
ground almonds and half the
coriander leaves and cook,
uncovered, for 2-3 minutes.
Remove the pan from the heat
and add the lemon juice, then
mix well. Garnish with the
remaining coriander leaves and
scatter the crushed pistachio nuts
over the curry.

# KOFTA (MEATBALL) CURRY

*Meatballs are popular throughout India. I always make them with finely minced meat as they stay together better than those made with coarse mince.*

Serves 4

## INGREDIENTS

### For the Koftas
460g/1lb lean minced lamb
2 cloves garlic, peeled and chopped
1.25cm/½ inch piece of fresh root ginger, peeled and roughly chopped
1 small onion, roughly chopped
60ml/2 fl oz water
1 fresh green chilli, seeded and chopped
2 tbsps freshly chopped coriander leaves
1 tbsp freshly chopped mint leaves
1 tsp salt

### For the Sauce or Gravy
5 tbsps cooking oil
2 onions, finely chopped
1.25cm/½ inch piece of fresh root ginger, peeled and grated
2 cloves garlic, peeled and crushed
2 tsps ground coriander
1½ tsps ground cumin
½ tsp ground turmeric
¼-½ tsp chilli powder
200g/7oz can tomatoes
150ml/¼ pint warm water
½ tsp salt
2 brown cardamom pods, opened
4 whole cloves
5cm/2 inch piece cinnamon stick, broken up
2 bay leaves, crushed
2 tbsps thick-set natural yogurt
2 tbsps ground almonds
1 tbsp freshly chopped coriander leaves

Place half the mince, all the garlic, ginger, onion and water in a saucepan over a medium heat. Bring slowly to the boil, then cover and simmer until all liquid evaporates in 30-35 minutes. Cook uncovered, if necessary, to dry out any excess liquid. Combine the cooked mince with the rest of the kofta ingredients, including the raw mince. Place the mixture into a liquidiser or food processor and blend until smooth. Chill the mixture for 30 minutes.

Divide the meat mixture into approximately 20 pieces, each slightly bigger than a walnut. Roll them between your hands to make neat round koftas.

Heat the oil for the sauce over a medium heat and fry the onions until they are just soft. Add the ginger and garlic and fry for 1 minute, then add the coriander, cumin, turmeric and chilli powder and stir quickly. Add one tomato at a time to the spice mixture with a little of the juice, stirring until the mixture begins to look dry. Add the water, salt, cardamoms, cloves, cinnamon and the bay leaves. Stir once and add the koftas. Bring to the boil, cover and simmer for 5 minutes.

Beat the yogurt with a fork until smooth, add the ground almonds and beat again. Stir gently into the curry, cover and simmer until the koftas are firm. Stir the curry gently, cover again, and simmer for a further 10-15 minutes, stirring occasionally to ensure that the thickened sauce or gravy does not stick to the pan. Stir in half the coriander leaves and serve.

# SIKANDARI RAAN
# (ROASTED SPICED LAMB
# AND POTATOES)

*This is a wonderful way to roast a leg of lamb. The meat is marinated for 48 hours before being cooked, coated with a yogurt and cashew nut paste.*

Serves 6-8

### INGREDIENTS
1.6-1.8kg/3½-4lb leg of lamb

280g/10oz thick-set natural
  yogurt
2.5cm/1 inch piece of fresh root
  ginger, peeled and roughly
  chopped
4-6 cloves garlic, peeled and
  roughly chopped
1 onion, roughly chopped
1 fresh green chilli
2 tbsps freshly chopped mint *or* 1
  tsp dried or bottled mint

1 tbsp ground coriander
1 tsp ground cumin

1 tsp garam masala
1 tsp ground turmeric
1¼ tsps salt or to taste

2 tbsps white poppy seeds
1 tbsp sesame seeds
2 tbsps desiccated coconut

30g/1oz ghee or unsalted butter
460g/1lb potatoes, peeled and
  halved

150g/5 oz thick-set natural yogurt
60g/2oz raw cashews
60g/2oz seedless raisins, soaked
  in a little warm water for 30
  minutes

Trim as much fat as possible from the meat. Make deep incisions from top to bottom at about 6mm/¼ inch intervals. These incisions should be as deep as possible, almost down to the bone. Turn the leg over and repeat the process. Blend the yogurt with the ginger, garlic, onion, green chilli and mint in a liquidiser or food processor, until smooth. Add the ground spices and salt and blend again. Grind the poppy and sesame seeds with the coconut and add this to the spiced yogurt. Rub the mixture over the lamb, forcing it into the incisions. Place in a covered container and leave to marinate in the refrigerator for 48 hours. Turn the meat every 12 hours.

Preheat the oven to 230°C/450°F/Gas Mark 8. Place the leg of lamb in a roasting tin, melt the ghee or butter and pour it over the meat. Cover the meat with aluminium foil or use a covered roasting dish and cook in the centre of the oven for 20 minutes. Reduce the temperature to 190°C/375°F/Gas Mark 5 and cook for a further 30 minutes. Add the potatoes and spoon some of the spiced yogurt over them as well as over the meat. Cover and cook for a further 35-40 minutes, basting the meat and the potatoes occasionally with more of the yogurt.

Blend the remaining yogurt with the cashews and raisins in a liquidiser or food processor until smooth. Pour the liquidised nut mixture over the meat, cover and return the meat to the oven for about 30 minutes, basting the meat and the potatoes as before. Transfer the meat to a warmed serving dish and arrange the potatoes around it. Spoon any remaining liquid over the meat and the potatoes. Serve the meat cut into chunky pieces rather than thin slices.

# ROGAN JOSH

*Rogan Josh is spicy yet creamy, a rich blend of lamb, tomatoes and seasonings. It is one of my favourite restaurant curries.*

Serves 4-6

## INGREDIENTS

40g/1½oz ghee or unsalted butter

1kg/2¼lbs boneless leg of lamb, cut into 4cm/1½ inch cubes

1 tbsp ground cumin

1 tbsp ground coriander

1 tsp ground turmeric

1 tsp chilli powder

2.5cm/1 inch piece of fresh root ginger, peeled and grated

2-4 cloves garlic, peeled and crushed

225g-275g/8-10oz onions, finely sliced

400g/14oz can tomatoes, chopped or whole

1 tbsp tomato purée

120ml/4 fl oz warm water

1¼ tsps salt

90ml/3 fl oz double cream

2 tsps garam masala

2 tbsps freshly chopped coriander leaves

Melt 30g/1oz of the ghee or butter over a medium heat and fry the meat in 2-3 batches until it changes colour. Remove each batch from the pan with a slotted spoon and set to one side. Turn the heat as low as possible and then add the cumin, coriander, turmeric, chilli powder, ginger and garlic. Stir and fry for 30 seconds. Increase the heat again to medium and add the meat with all its juices. Stir and fry for 3-4 minutes then add the onions. Fry for 5-6 minutes stirring frequently, then add the tomatoes and tomato purée and cook for 2-3 minutes. Add the water and salt, bring to the boil, cover and simmer until the meat is tender, for about 60 minutes. Stir in the cream and remove the pan from the heat.

In a separate pan melt the remaining ghee over a medium heat and add the garam masala, stir briskly and add to the meat. Transfer a little meat gravy to the pan in which the garam masala was fried – stir thoroughly to ensure that any remaining garam masala and ghee mixture is fully incorporated into the gravy and add this to the meat. Mix well. Stir in the coriander leaves, then serve.

# KASHMIRI LAMB KABABS

*These kababs are easy to prepare and will benefit from as
long a marinade as you can give them – the longer the
marinade, the tastier the meat. Cook the kababs on the
barbecue in the summer.*

Serves 4

*INGREDIENTS*

680g/1½ lbs boneless lamb,
  shoulder or leg
2 tbsps oil
1 clove garlic, peeled and
  crushed
1 tbsp ground cumin
1 tsp turmeric
1 tsp fresh root ginger, peeled
  and grated
Freshly chopped coriander or
  parsley leaves
Salt and freshly ground black
  pepper
1 red pepper, seeded and cut in
  2.5cm/1 inch pieces
1 small onion, cut in rings

Cut the lamb into 2.5cm/1 inch
cubes. Heat the oil and cook the
garlic, cumin, turmeric and
ginger for 1 minute, then add the
coriander, salt and pepper. Allow
to cool, then rub the spice
mixture over the meat. Leave
covered in the refrigerator for
several hours.

Thread the meat onto skewers,
alternating it with the pepper
pieces. Cook for about 10
minutes under a preheated grill,
turning frequently. During the
last 5 minutes, thread sliced
onion rings around the meat and
continue cooking until the onion
is cooked and lightly browned
and the meat is cooked to your
preference.

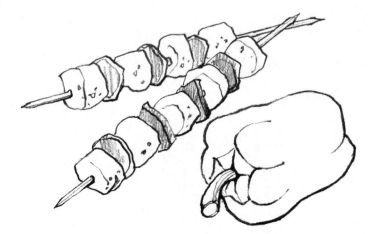

# DAM KE KABAB
# (BAKED KABAB)

*This is so simple to make and utterly delicious! The spiced mince is baked and then cut into pieces. Serve as a main course or, cut into small pieces and threaded onto cocktail sticks, as a savoury appetiser.*

Serves 4

### INGREDIENTS

460g/1lb lean minced beef or lamb
1 tsp fresh root ginger, peeled and grated
2-3 cloves garlic, peeled and crushed
2 green chillies, ground or finely chopped
2 tsps garam masala
150ml/¼ pint natural yogurt
¼ tsp meat tenderiser (optional)
1 tbsp freshly chopped coriander
1 tsp chilli powder
2 eggs, lightly beaten
1 onion, thinly sliced and fried until crisp
Salt
Oil
2 green chillies, chopped
Juice of 1 lemon

Preheat the oven to 180°C/350°F/Gas Mark 4. Mix together the mince, ginger, garlic, ground chilli, garam masala, yogurt, meat tenderiser, half the finely chopped coriander, the chilli powder, eggs and crisply fried onions. Stir well and season with salt. Spread the mince over a well greased baking tray – it should be 1.25cm/½ inch thick. Brush with oil and bake in the preheated oven for 20 minutes. Reduce the temperature to 150°C/300°F/Gas Mark 2 and cook for a further 20-30 minutes, or until any liquid has evaporated. Cut the mince into 5cm/2 inch squares. Garnish with the remaining chopped chillies and fresh coriander. Sprinkle with lemon juice before serving.

# SAVOURY MINCE & EGGS

*The eggs are baked on a bed of spiced minced meat to provide an economical and filling family dish. I always lightly prick the egg yolks before baking, which prevents them from splitting.*

Serves 4-6

## INGREDIENTS

4 tbsps cooking oil
1 large onion, roughly chopped
2.5cm/1 inch piece of fresh root ginger, peeled and roughly chopped
4-6 cloves garlic, peeled and roughly chopped
150g/5oz thick-set natural yogurt
1 tsp cumin seeds
1 tsp ground turmeric
1 tsp ground coriander
460g/1lb lean minced beef or lamb
1 tsp paprika
280ml/½ pint warm water
1 tsp salt
1 tbsp tomato purée
½ tsp garam masala
2 tbsps freshly chopped coriander leaves
4-6 small eggs (1 per person)

Heat 2 tbsps of oil over a medium heat and fry the onion, ginger and garlic for 3-4 minutes, stirring frequently. Remove from the heat and allow to cool slightly. Place the yogurt and fried onion mixture in a liquidiser or food processor and blend until smooth. Set aside.

Heat the remaining oil and fry the cumin seeds until they pop. Remove the pan from the heat and add the turmeric and coriander, stir and mix thoroughly. Adding the spices off the heat prevents them from burning. Place the pan back on the heat and add the mince. Fry over a medium heat until the mince is lightly browned and completely dry. Add the paprika, water and salt, bring to the boil, cover and simmer for 15 minutes. Stir occasionally.

Preheat the oven to 190°C/375°F/Gas Mark 5. Add the blended yogurt and onion and the tomato purée, return to the boil, cover and simmer for a further 15 minutes. Stir occasionally. Stir in the garam masala and the coriander leaves, then remove the pan from the heat. Turn the mince into an ovenproof dish, making 4-6 hollows, according to the number of eggs to be used, about 2.5cm/1 inch apart. Break an egg into each hollow; do not worry about the egg white spilling over. Bake in the centre of the oven for 30 minutes or until the eggs are set. Bake for a few minutes longer if you like the yolks hard. Garnish with the remaining coriander leaves before serving.

# KHEEMA-PALAK
# (MINCE WITH SPINACH)

*I have only recently realised that minced meat is seldom
cooked by itself in India – most classic curries made with
mince include a second main ingredient, either a vegetable
or eggs. One of the most popular vegetables for curry –
spinach – is used in this dish.*

Serves 4-6

### INGREDIENTS
4 tbsps cooking oil
½ tsp black mustard seeds
1 tsp cumin seeds
1 fresh green chilli, finely
  chopped, seeded if a milder
  flavour is preferred
2.5cm/1 inch piece of fresh root
  ginger, peeled and finely
  grated
6 cloves garlic, peeled and
  crushed
460g/1lb lean minced beef or
  lamb
1 large onion, finely sliced
2 cinnamon sticks, 5cm/2 inches
  long, broken up
½ tsp ground turmeric
1 tbsp ground cumin
½ tsp ground black pepper
340g/12oz fresh spinach leaves,
  chopped *or* 225g/8oz frozen
  spinach, defrosted and drained
1 tsp salt
200g/7oz can tomatoes, drained
  and chopped, *or* 3-4 ripe
  tomatoes, skinned and
  chopped
1 tsp garam masala

Heat 2 tbsps of oil in a wide
shallow pan over a medium heat
and fry the mustard seeds until
they crackle. Add the cumin
seeds, green chilli, ginger and
half the garlic. Stir and fry for 30
seconds. Add the mince and
cook until all the liquid
evaporates – this will take 8-10
minutes. Remove the pan from
the heat and set aside.

Heat the remaining oil in a
separate pan over a medium heat
and stir in the remaining garlic.
Add the onions and cinnamon
sticks and fry until the onions are
lightly browned, stirring
frequently. Reduce the heat and
add the turmeric, cumin and
black pepper. Stir and fry for 1
minute, then add the spinach and
mix thoroughly. Add the mince
and stir until the spinach and the
mince are thoroughly mixed.
Cover the pan and simmer for 15
minutes. Increase the heat
slightly, add the salt and the
tomatoes, stir and cook for 2-3
minutes. Add the garam masala,
and cook for a further 2-3
minutes. Remove the pan from
the heat, add a little extra salt
and pepper if necessary, and
serve.

# KHEEMA SHAHZADA

*Kheema is the Indian word for minced meat. The best mince for curries should be lean but quite coarse – ground steak is really too fine.*

Serves 4

## INGREDIENTS
90g/3oz ghee or unsalted butter
1 large onion, roughly chopped
2.5cm/1 inch piece of fresh root ginger, peeled and roughly chopped
2-4 cloves garlic, peeled and roughly chopped

1 cinnamon stick, 5cm/2 inches long, broken up
4 green cardamoms
4 whole cloves
4-6 dried red chillies
1 tbsp coriander seeds

1 tbsp white poppy seeds
1 tbsp sesame seeds

460g/1lb lean minced beef or lamb
½ tsp ground turmeric
60g/2oz raw cashews, split into halves
1 tsp salt
280ml/½ pint warm water
150ml/¼ pint milk
2 hard-boiled eggs, quartered lengthways
Few sprigs of fresh coriander

Melt half the ghee or butter over a medium heat and fry the onions, ginger and garlic until the onions are soft. Squeeze out any excess fat by pressing the fried ingredients onto the side of the pan with a wooden spatula, then transfer them to a plate and allow to cool. Grind the two separate groups of spices and seeds. Add the remaining ghee or butter to the pan and fry the ground spices and seeds for 1 minute, stirring constantly. Add the mince and fry until all the liquid evaporates in about 10 minutes, stirring frequently, then add the turmeric, stir and fry for 30 seconds. Stir in the salt, cashews and the water, then bring to the boil, cover the pan and cook over a low heat for 15 minutes, stirring occasionally.

Meanwhile, pour the milk into a liquidiser or food processor and add the fried onions, garlic and ginger. Blend until smooth and stir into the mince. Return to the boil, cover the pan and simmer for 10-15 minutes or until the sauce is thick. Transfer the mince to a warmed serving dish and garnish with the hard-boiled eggs and coriander leaves.

# KHEEMA MATTAR
# (CURRIED MINCE & PEAS)

*Keema means mince and mattar peas, so this might sound like a typical curried mince. Not so – the spices and ground almonds turn it into a delicious curry.*

Serves 4

*INGREDIENTS*
6 tbsp cooking oil
1 tsp cumin seeds
2 dried red chillies
460g/1lb lean minced beef or lamb
1 large onion, finely chopped
2.5cm/1 inch piece of fresh root ginger, peeled and finely grated
4 cloves garlic, peeled and crushed
½ tsp ground turmeric
2 tsps ground coriander
1½ tsps ground cumin
½ tsp chilli powder
200g/7oz can tomatoes, or 3-4 fresh tomatoes, skinned and chopped
1 tsp salt
1 tbsp natural yogurt
175ml/6 fl oz warm water
120g/4oz fresh or frozen peas, shelled weight
1 tbsp ground almonds
½ tsp garam masala
2 hard-boiled eggs, sliced
2 tbsps freshly chopped coriander leaves

Heat 1 tbsp of oil over a medium heat and add the cumin seeds. As soon as they pop add the red chillies and then the mince. Stir and cook until the mince is evenly browned. Meanwhile, heat the remaining oil in a large pan over a medium heat and add the onions. Fry until the onions are soft, then add the ginger and garlic and cook for a further 2-3 minutes. Stir in the turmeric and then the coriander, cumin and chilli powder. Add the tomatoes with all the juice, stir and cook for a further 3-4 minutes. Add the browned mince and cook for 6-8 minutes, stirring frequently. Stir in the salt and water and then the yogurt. Cover the pan and simmer for 20 minutes.

Add the peas and simmer for a further 10 minutes. If using fresh peas, boil them until tender before adding to the mince. Stir in the ground almonds and simmer for 2-3 minutes then remove the pan from the heat and stir in the garam masala. Transfer to a warmed serving dish and arrange the sliced eggs on top. Garnish with the coriander leaves.

# KOFTA (MEATBALL) BHOONA

*A curry of meatballs will always have the word 'kofta' in its title. You only need a tiny piece of root ginger for this recipe – 6mm/¼ inch is plenty.*

Serves 4-6

## INGREDIENTS

460g/1lb fine lean minced beef or lamb
1 large clove of garlic, peeled and crushed
1 tsp garam masala
1-2 fresh green chillies, seeded and minced
2 tbsps fresh coriander leaves, minced
1½ tsps salt
3 tbsps cooking oil
1 large onion, finely chopped
Small piece of fresh root ginger, peeled and grated
2 tsps ground coriander
1 tsp ground cumin

### Spice Paste

½-1 tsp chilli powder
2 cloves garlic, peeled and crushed
½ tsp ground turmeric
2 tbsps tomato purée
120ml/4 fl oz cold water

225ml/8 fl oz warm water
60g/2oz frozen peas
¼ tsp garam masala
2 tbsps freshly chopped coriander leaves

Place the mince in a large bowl and add the garlic, garam masala, green chillies, 1 tsp salt and the coriander leaves. Mix the ingredients thoroughly and knead the mince until it is smooth. Divide the mixture into about 28-30 marble-sized balls (koftas), rolling them between the palms of your hands.

Heat the oil over a medium heat, preferably in a non-stick or cast iron pan, and fry the koftas in 2-3 batches. Turn the koftas as they brown and, when they are brown all over, remove them with a slotted spoon and drain on absorbent kitchen paper. In the same oil, fry the onions and ginger until the onions are golden brown, stirring frequently. Reduce the heat to low and add the ground coriander. Fry for 30 seconds then add the ground cumin and fry for a further 30 seconds. Increase the heat to medium and add 2 tbsps of the spice paste. Stir and fry until it dries up. Repeat the process until all the spice paste is used up. Add the warm water and the remaining salt and bring to the boil, then add the koftas, cover the pan and simmer for 10 minutes.

Increase the heat to medium, and bring the bhoona to the boil, stir and cook for 4-5 minutes. Add the peas and the garam masala and continue to cook, uncovered, until the sauce is fairly thick, stirring frequently. Stir in the coriander leaves, add a little more salt if necessary and serve.

# KHEEMA-SALI MATTAR

*The Parsees, ancient Persians, settled in India and contributed some wonderful dishes to the classic cuisine of their adopted country. Some of my favourite curries are, like this rich mince dish, Parsi in origin. Parsi dishes are often garnished with fried potato sticks.*

Serves 4-6

### INGREDIENTS

5 tbsps cooking oil
1 tsp cumin seeds
1 large onion, finely chopped
1.25cm/½ inch piece of fresh root ginger, peeled and finely grated
3-4 cloves garlic, peeled and crushed
½ tsp ground turmeric
1 tsp ground cinnamon
½ tsp ground nutmeg
1 tsp ground mixed spice
2 tsps ground coriander
½ tsp chilli powder
460g/1lb lean coarse minced beef or lamb
200g/7oz can tomatoes
1 tsp salt
150ml/¼ pint warm water
2 tbsps natural yogurt
175g/6oz frozen peas or shelled fresh peas, boiled until tender
2 tbsps freshly chopped coriander leaves
2 tbsps ghee or unsalted butter
340g/12oz potatoes, peeled and cut into matchstick strips
¼ tsp salt
¼ tsp chilli powder

Heat the oil over a medium heat and fry the cumin seeds until they pop. Add the onions, ginger and garlic and fry until the onions are golden brown. Add the turmeric, cinnamon, nutmeg, mixed spice, coriander and chilli powder, stir and fry on a low heat for 2-3 minutes. Stir in the mince and fry until the mince is brown and all the liquid has evaporated. Add the tomatoes and cook for 2-3 minutes stirring frequently, then add the salt and water. Bring to the boil, cover and cook on a low heat for 15-20 minutes.

Beat the yogurt until it is smooth and add it to the mince with the peas. Return to the boil, cover and simmer for 5 minutes. Stir in half the coriander leaves and remove the pan from the heat.

Melt the ghee or butter over a medium heat in a non-stick or cast iron pan and fry the potato sticks in a single layer until they are well browned and tender, reducing the heat as the potato starts to cook. You will need to do this in 2-3 batches. Drain the potato sticks on absorbent kitchen paper. Season the potato sticks with the salt and chilli powder. Place the mince in the middle of a serving dish and arrange the potato sticks around it. Garnish with the remaining coriander leaves.

# CAULIFLOWER SURPRISE

*This doesn't sound like an authentic name for a classic Indian recipe! However, it is an unusual and imaginative way of serving cauliflower, stuffed with minced beef or lamb.*

Serves 4

## INGREDIENTS

1 cauliflower
4 tbsps cooking oil
1 tsp cumin seeds
1 large onion, finely chopped
2.5cm/1 inch piece of fresh root ginger, peeled and grated
3-4 cloves garlic, peeled and crushed
460g/1lb lean minced beef or lamb
1 tsp ground turmeric
1 tbsp ground coriander
1 tsp ground cinnamon
1 tsp ground cardamom seeds
½ tsp chilli powder
200g/7oz can tomatoes, drained
1 tsp salt
¼ tsp black mustard seeds
½ tsp cumin seeds
8-10 curry leaves

### To Garnish

2 small tomatoes, quartered
1 tbsp freshly chopped coriander leaves

Blanch the whole cauliflower in boiling salted water, then drain and cool. Heat 3 tbsps of oil over a medium heat and add the cumin seeds. As soon as the seeds start popping, add the onion and fry for 3-4 minutes, stirring frequently. Add the ginger and garlic, stir and fry for 1 minute. Add the mince, increase the heat slightly, stir and fry the mince until it is crumbly and all the liquid has evaporated.

Reduce the heat to low and add the turmeric, coriander, cinnamon, cardamom and chilli powder. Stir and fry until the spices are well-blended in 3-4 minutes. Add the tomatoes and salt, stir and cook for 1-2 minutes. Cover the pan and simmer for a further 10-15 minutes, then remove the pan from the heat and allow the mince to cool.

Place the cauliflower on a board, stem side up. Fill all the cavity between the stems with the cooked mince; this should be as tightly packed as possible. Turn the cauliflower over, gently pull the florets apart and fill with as much mince as possible. Heat the remaining oil over a medium heat and add the mustard seeds. As soon as the seeds pop, add the cumin and the curry leaves. Place the cauliflower in the seasoned oil, the right way up, and let it cook, uncovered, for 2-3 minutes. Turn it over and cook the other side for 2-3 minutes. Turn the cauliflower over again and arrange any remaining mince around it. Cover the pan and lower the heat to the minimum setting. Cook for 10-15 minutes or until the cauliflower is tender.

Place the cauliflower on a warmed serving dish and arrange any surplus mince around it. Garnish with the tomatoes and coriander leaves.

# KEEMA METHI (MINCE WITH FENUGREEK)

*Methi is the Indian word for fenugreek. It is easy to find in seeds or ground, but you may have to visit an Indian grocer to find the leaves.*

Serves 4

### INGREDIENTS

1 onion, chopped
30g/1oz ghee *or* 2 tbsps oil
4 small green cardamoms
2.5cm/1 inch cinnamon stick
1 bay leaf
6 cloves
1 tsp fresh root ginger, peeled and grated
2-3 cloves garlic, peeled and crushed
460g/1lb minced beef or lamb
1 tsp chilli powder
2 tsps ground coriander
2 tsps ground cumin
¼ tsp ground turmeric
150ml/¼ pint natural yogurt
Salt
1 bunch fresh methi (fenugreek) leaves, stemmed and chopped *or* 1 tbsp dry kasuri methi leaves

Fry the onion in the ghee or oil until soft, then add the cardamoms, cinnamon stick, bay leaf and cloves and fry for 1 minute. Add the ginger and garlic and cook for 1 minute, then add the mince. Stir the mixture and add the chilli, coriander, cumin and turmeric. Mix well and cook for 5 minutes. Beat the yogurt with the methi and add it to the pan. Cover and cook until the liquid is absorbed. Season with salt to taste before serving.

# GOAN CURRY

*Goa, a state of western India, formerly part of Portuguese India, is now a very popular holiday resort. This curry is typical of the food of the area – coconut is one of the principal crops.*

Serves 4

### INGREDIENTS

60g/2oz ghee *or* 3 tbsps oil
1 large onion, chopped
1 bay leaf
2.5cm/1 inch cinnamon stick
5 green cardamoms
6 cloves
3 cloves garlic, peeled and crushed
1 tsp fresh root ginger, peeled and grated
8 curry leaves
460g/1lb lean pork, diced
1 tbsp tamarind pulp
150ml/¼ pint natural yogurt
¼ tsp ground turmeric
1 tsp freshly ground black pepper
1 tsp ground cumin
1 tsp ground coriander
½ tsp sugar
1 tbsp desiccated coconut
Salt
150ml/¼ pint water
1 tbsp freshly chopped coriander
2 green chillies, chopped

Heat the ghee or oil and fry the onion until golden brown. Add the bay leaf, cinnamon, cardamoms, cloves, garlic, ginger and curry leaves and fry for 1-2 minutes. Add the pork and fry for 5-7 minutes, until all the juice has evaporated. Add the tamarind pulp, yogurt, turmeric, black pepper, cumin, coriander, sugar, coconut and salt to taste. Mix well, cover and cook for 20-30 minutes. Add a little extra water if the mixture is too dry.

Add the chopped coriander and chilli, cover and cook for 20-25 minutes, or until pork is tender. The dish should have a smooth gravy.

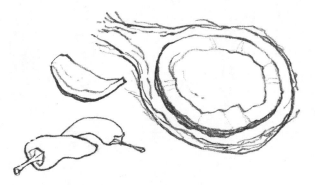

# TALI KALEJI/GURDA/DIL (MIXED FRY)

*Not everyone likes offal but this curry brings out the richness
of the meat. Serve with rice or chapatis and an Indian salad
or raita.*

Serves 4

### INGREDIENTS
225g/8oz pig's liver, cut into
   small dice
4 lambs' kidneys, halved and
   cored
2 hearts, cored and cut into
   2.5cm/1 inch pieces
Salt
1 tsp chilli powder
2 tsps ground coriander
¼ tsp ground turmeric
2-3 cloves garlic peeled and
   crushed
1 tsp fresh root ginger, peeled
   and finely grated
40g/1½oz ghee *or* 3 tbsps oil
1 lemon

Rinse all the meats in lightly
salted water and remove any fat
and sinew. Drain well and toss in
the chilli powder, coriander,
turmeric and garlic, then set
aside for 5 minutes.

Melt the ghee or oil in a large
saucepan and add the meat
mixture. Cook gently for 40-45
minutes, stirring occasionally.
Add salt to taste. The colour will
change to a rich dark brown.
When the mixture is dry and the
oil separates, remove from the
heat and sprinkle with lemon
juice. If the meats become too
dry during cooking, add a little
water or stock.

# PULSES, RICE & BREADS

Pulse vegetables are essential to classic Indian cooking, and to the everyday fare of the vast majority of Indian people. They are served as an accompaniment to meat or chicken dishes in wealthier households, but for many thousands of Indians they are their staple food, eaten daily and very often for two meals a day. For those who cannot afford to eat meat or who have adopted a vegetarian diet for religious reasons, pulses are their main source of protein and also provide a useful amount of B group vitamins.

## A Variety of Flavours

My one criticism of cooking with pulse vegetables is that the resulting dishes so often taste the same, whatever pulse has been used. It is a challenge to a cook to produce tasty and interesting dishes with pulse vegetables and the Indians have a classic tradition of doing so through their imaginative and innovative use of spices. Most dhals are spiced in some way – some have a garnish of spices roasted in ghee or butter poured over them just before serving, in the same way as a Mediterranean cook might pour a little extra virgin olive oil over a dish at the last moment.

A dhal may be as spicy or mild as you like. Very bland dhals are given to young children and invalids, providing a nutritious and easily digestible meal. Others may be so highly spiced that they would dominate most curries and are served simply with plain rice or breads.

## Get Organised!

Most dried pulse vegetables require soaking before use, otherwise they simply will not cook soft. The best way to soak is in cold water for a minimum of 8 hours or overnight. If you are really in a hurry, add boiling water and then cook the covered pulses in a large covered bowl in a microwave, for 10 minutes on full power, and then leave them for just one hour. This provides a reasonable soak – but is not a classic Indian technique! Red lentils are one of the few pulses which do not require soaking and they cook very quickly, making them an invaluable store cupboard ingredient.

## Rice – Basic Rules for Success

I wish to pass on a few tips for successful rice cookery. A whole meal may be marred by a dish of gelatinous grains stuck together in a lump, so it is important to perfect the art of cooking rice.

Most Indian dishes are best when cooked with Basmati rice, a fine long-grain of delicate flavour. It must, however, be thoroughly washed to remove all the excess starch before it is cooked, otherwise not only will it stick together, it will also boil over and make a frightful mess of your cooker. Place the rice in a sieve and wash it under cold water until the water runs clear – this may take up to 5 minutes.

## The Less Fuss the Better

Do not fiddle with rice during cooking – leave it to its own devices. Bring it to the boil in the prescribed amount of water with a pinch of salt in an open pan and then stir it once to prevent it from sticking to the bottom of the pan. Cover the pan tightly and cook for the recommended time, then remove the pan from the heat and leave it, covered and undisturbed, for a minimum of 10 minutes. Fork through the rice gently before serving to separate the grains and you should have a perfect result. If you are not following a recipe which gives quantities for rice and water, cook one measure of rice with two of water – the rice will absorb all the water as it cooks.

## Flat Breads for Feasting

Most Indian breads are unleavened, and are therefore relatively quick to cook. The exceptions are naan and batura, a rich dough made with egg and yogurt. Many breads are cooked in a dry pan, although some are baked or fried.

Chapatis and naan are both available in supermarkets and are useful standbys when time is short. There can, however, be no substitute for making your own Indian breads. I think this is especially true of naan as I like to flavour them either with sultanas, slivered almonds and spices, or a little spiced minced beef or lamb.

A meal of bread, dhal and raita or salad may not sound very exciting but, when the dhal and the breads are both home-made, such a meal is a veritable feast combining delightful flavours and textures.

# RAZMA (RED KIDNEY BEAN CURRY)

*Red kidney beans make a colourful, tasty curry. Remember to boil them rapidly for 10 minutes at the start of their cooking period to destroy any toxins in the beans.*

Serves 4

### INGREDIENTS
225g/8oz red kidney beans, washed
570ml/1 pint water
1 tsp bicarbonate of soda
60g/2oz ghee *or* 3 tbsps oil
1 onion, chopped
2.5cm/1 inch cinnamon stick
1 bay leaf
3 brown cardamoms
1 tsp fresh root ginger, peeled and finely grated
4 cloves garlic, peeled and crushed
1 tsp chilli powder
1 tsp ground coriander
1 tsp garam masala
¼ tsp turmeric
200g/7oz can chopped tomatoes
Salt to taste
2 green chillies, halved
1 tbsp freshly chopped coriander leaves

Soak the kidney beans in the water with bicarbonate of soda overnight. Drain the beans, rinse and boil in fresh water for 1 hour or until the beans are cooked. Cool and strain the beans, retaining the cooking liquid.

Heat the ghee or oil and fry the onion for 2-3 minutes. Add the cinnamon, bay leaf, cardamoms, ginger and garlic. Cook for 1 minute then add the chilli powder, ground coriander, garam masala and turmeric. Stir the spices well. Add the tomatoes and salt, then the kidney beans and fry the mixture for 2-3 minutes. Add 175-225ml/6-8 fl oz of the bean cooking liquor, the green chilli and chopped coriander. Simmer for 15-20 minutes. Add more bean liquor if the sauce is too thick. Transfer the Razma to a warmed dish and serve.

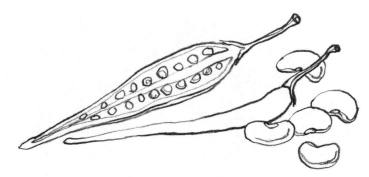

# ALOO CHOLE

*Use canned chick peas to make this dish if you are in a hurry – they will not provide the same texture as freshly cooked chick peas but are a good stand-by in the store cupboard.*

Serves 4-6

## INGREDIENTS

225g/8oz chick peas, picked over and washed
850ml/1½ pints water
1.25cm/½ inch piece of fresh root ginger, peeled and grated
1 large potato, peeled and cut into 4cm/1½ inch dice
1 tsp ground cumin
½ tsp ground turmeric
¼-½ tsp chilli powder, optional
1-2 fresh green chillies, slit lengthways into halves, seeded for a milder flavour
30g/1oz ghee or unsalted butter
1 large onion, finely chopped
1¼ tsps salt
½ tsp garam masala
1 tbsp lemon juice
1 tbsp freshly chopped fresh mint *or* 1 tsp dried mint

Soak the chick peas overnight in plenty of cold water. Rinse several times and drain well. Place the chick peas, water and ginger in a large saucepan over a high heat, bring to the boil, cover the pan and simmer for 1¼-1½ hours or until the chick peas are tender. Add the potato, cumin, turmeric, chilli powder and the green chillies and mint, if you are using dried. Return to the boil, cover the pan and simmer for a further 15-20 minutes, until the potatoes are tender.

Melt the ghee over a medium heat and fry the onions until they are lightly browned. Stir them into the chick peas with the salt and garam masala. Remove the pan from the heat and stir in the lemon juice and fresh mint. Serve immediately.

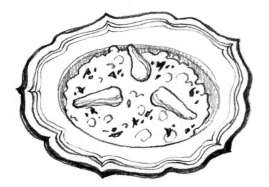

# LOBIA CURRY (BLACK EYED BEAN CURRY)

*A bean curry with a thick tomato sauce, ideal to serve with brown rice and salad.*

Serves 4

## INGREDIENTS

225g/8oz lobia (black-eye beans), washed and soaked overnight in water
570ml/1 pint water
1 onion, chopped
60g/2oz ghee *or* 3 tbsps oil
1 bay leaf
2.5cm/1 inch cinnamon stick
1 tsp fresh root ginger, peeled and grated
2-3 cloves garlic, peeled and crushed
¼ tsp ground turmeric
1 tsp ground coriander
1 tsp chilli powder
4-5 canned tomatoes, crushed *or* 4 fresh tomatoes, chopped
Salt
2 green chillies, halved and chopped
2 tbsp freshly chopped coriander

Boil the soaked beans in the water for 20 minutes, then allow them to cool. Fry the onion in the ghee or oil for 3-4 minutes. Add the bay leaf, cinnamon, ginger and garlic and fry for 2 minutes, then add the turmeric, ground coriander, chilli powder and stir well. Add the beans, tomatoes, salt, chopped chilli and coriander. Cover and simmer for 10-15 minutes.

# CHANA MASALA

*This is a medium hot curry of chick peas – use canned chick peas if time is short. You will need two 430g/12oz cans, drained.*

Serves 4

### INGREDIENTS

1 large onion, chopped
4 cloves garlic, peeled and crushed
2.5cm/1 inch piece fresh root ginger, peeled and finely chopped
3 tbsps ghee
1 tbsp ground coriander
2 tsps cumin seeds
¼ tsp cayenne pepper
1 tsp turmeric
2 tsps ground cumin
1 tbsp amchur (dried mango powder) *or* 1 tbsp lemon juice
2 tsps paprika
400g/14oz can tomatoes
680g/1½ lbs cooked chick peas (340g/12oz uncooked)
1 tsp garam masala
½ tsp salt
1 fresh green chilli, finely chopped

Cook the onion, garlic and ginger in the ghee until soft. Add all the spices and fry over a low heat for 1-2 minutes, stirring all the time. Add the tomatoes, roughly chopped, together with their juice, then add the cooked chick peas. Cook for 30 minutes over a medium heat.

Add the garam masala, salt and chopped chilli, stir well and serve hot.

# SAAGWALLA DHAL

*This dhal is very green in colour and not very attractive to the eye, but the flavour is delicious. Serve topped with yogurt for a more attractive presentation.*

Serves 6-8

### INGREDIENTS

175g/6oz skinless split moong dhal *or* yellow split peas
30g/1oz ghee or unsalted butter
1 large onion, finely sliced
1 fresh green chilli, sliced lengthways; seeded for a milder flavour
2 cinnamon sticks, 5cm/2 inches long, broken up into 2-3 pieces
½ tsp ground turmeric
½ tsp garam masala
¼ tsp chilli powder
1 tsp salt
1 tsp ground cumin
2 ripe tomatoes, skinned and chopped
570ml/1 pint warm water
2 tbsps cooking oil
½ tsp black mustard seeds
2-3 cloves garlic, peeled and finely chopped
1-2 dried red chillies, roughly chopped
120g/4oz frozen leaf spinach, defrosted and finely chopped *or* 275g/10oz fresh spinach, hard stalks removed and finely chopped

Wash and soak the dhal for 1½-2 hours. Drain well. Melt the ghee or butter over a medium heat in a non-stick or cast iron pan and fry the onion, green chilli and cinnamon until the onion is lightly browned. Add the turmeric and garam masala, stir and mix well, then add the dhal, chilli powder and salt. Stir and fry for 8-10 minutes over a low heat. Add the cumin and tomatoes, and cook for 3-4 minutes, then add the water. Bring to the boil, cover and simmer for 30-35 minutes, stirring occasionally.

Meanwhile, heat the oil over a medium heat and fry the mustard seeds until they pop. Add the garlic and allow it to turn slightly brown, then add the dried red chillies and the spinach, and mix thoroughly. Cover the pan and simmer for 5 minutes. Add the spinach to the dhal, cover and cook over a low heat for 10 minutes, stirring occasionally. Serve with dry curries, topped with yogurt if liked.

# SAMBHAR (DHAL AND VEGETABLE)

*This is an unusual dhal, suitable for serving as a main course, as it contains plenty of fresh vegetables which give a colourful and attractive appearance.*

Serves 4

### INGREDIENTS

**Whole spices**
1 tsp coriander seeds
1 tsp cumin seeds
2 dry red chillies (whole)
2 tsp channa dhal
¼ tsp fenugreek seeds (methi)

225g/8oz toor dhal
570ml/1 pint water
1 carrot, peeled and sliced
1 potato, peeled and diced
6-8 okra (bhindi), topped and tailed and cut into 2.5cm/1 inch pieces
1 small courgette, sliced
1 small aubergine, halved and sliced
6 curry leaves
2 tbsps tamarind pulp
1 green chilli, cut in half
Salt to taste
1 sprig fresh green coriander
1 tbsp oil
½ tsp mustard seeds
¼ tsp asafoetida (hing)

Roast the spices until lightly browned in a dry frying pan over a low heat. Allow to cool, then grind in a pestle and mortar or a coffee grinder.

Wash the dhal in 4-5 changes of water, until the water is clear. Drain. Add 280ml/½ pint of water, cover and simmer gently for 6-10 minutes. Remove any froth that forms with a spoon. When the dhal is soft, beat it with a potato masher or whisk until smooth.

In a separate pan, boil the carrots, potatoes, aubergine, okra and courgette, with the ground, roasted spices and the remaining water for 4-5 minutes. Mix the dhal and vegetables with any remaining liquid. Add the curry leaves, tamarind pulp, salt, chopped chilli and fresh coriander. Simmer for 10-15 minutes, then turn into a warmed serving dish. Heat the oil and fry the mustard seeds and asafoetida for half a minute, then pour over the sambhar. Serve with boiled rice.

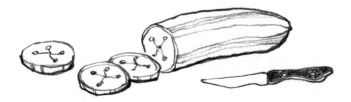

# KHARI URID DHAL
# (DRY URID DHAL)

*This is a dry dhal that may be served with paratha or any
Indian bread. Black beans are generally referred to as urid
dhal – without their husks or skins they are white.*

Serves 4

INGREDIENTS

225g/8oz white urid dhal,
   dehusked and washed in 3-4
   changes of water
Salt to taste
200ml/7 fl oz water

*For Garnish*
1 onion, sliced
60g/2oz unsalted butter
1 green chilli, chopped
2.5cm/1 inch fresh root ginger,
   peeled and sliced
.1 tbsp freshly chopped coriander

Cook the urid dhal in the water,
with salt to taste, over a low heat
until the water has evaporated.
Fry the onion in a separate pan
in the butter until golden brown.
Add the chopped chilli and
ginger and fry for 2-3 minutes.
Pour the onion mixture over the
dhal and garnish with the
chopped coriander.

# TARKA DHAL
# (SPICED LENTILS)

*At least one type of dhal is always served during an Indian meal. Dhals are of vital importance in the vegetarian diet, providing protein. I find that they are popular with everyone as they reduce the overall heat of the meal.*

Serves 4

### INGREDIENTS
175g/6oz masoor dhal (red split lentils)
700ml/1¼ pints water
1 tsp ground turmeric
1 tsp ground cumin
1 tsp salt
30g/1oz ghee or unsalted butter
1 onion, finely chopped
2 cloves garlic, peeled and finely chopped
2 dried red chillies, roughly chopped

Place the dhal, water, turmeric, cumin and salt in a saucepan and bring to the boil. Reduce the heat to medium and cook uncovered for 8-10 minutes, stirring frequently. Cover the pan and simmer for a further 30 minutes, stirring occasionally. Remove the dhal from the heat, allow it to cool slightly and then press through a sieve.

Melt the ghee or butter over a medium heat and fry the onion, garlic and red chillies until the onion is well browned. Stir half the fried onion into the dhal and turn it into a warmed serving dish. Arrange the remaining fried onions on top.

# MASOOR DHAL (RED LENTIL)

*Red lentils are widely available and are an excellent ingredient to keep in the store cupboard: they cook quickly and are high in protein.*

Serves 4

### INGREDIENTS
225g/8oz red lentils
570ml/1 pint water
1 tsp chilli powder
2 tsps ground coriander
¼ tsp turmeric powder
¼ tsp salt
1 tbsp freshly chopped coriander
4 fresh tomatoes, chopped *or* 5 canned tomatoes, crushed
1 onion, chopped
60g/2oz butter
1 green chilli, halved and chopped

Wash the lentils in 4-5 changes of water, until the water runs clear. Drain. Add 570ml/1 pint water and cover, then simmer gently, without stirring, for 10-15 minutes until the lentils are thoroughly cooked.

Blend the lentils with a masher or beat them with an egg beater. Add the chilli powder, ground coriander, turmeric, salt, fresh coriander and tomatoes, then cover and simmer for 6-8 minutes. Remove the pan from the heat. Fry the onion in the butter until brown then pour the onion and butter over the dhal. Garnish with the chopped chilli.

# SPICY CHANNA DHAL

*Channa Dhal is one of the best known side-dishes – it may also be made with yellow split peas. I like to serve it with kababs or any chicken dish.*

Serves 4-6

### INGREDIENTS

225g/8oz channa dhal or yellow split peas
45g/1½oz ghee or unsalted butter
1 large onion, finely sliced
2 cinnamon sticks, 5cm/2 inches long, broken up into 2-3 pieces
6 green cardamoms, the top of each pod split open
2-4 dried red chillies, roughly chopped
½ tsp ground turmeric
¼-½ tsp chilli powder
1¼ tsps salt
570ml/1 pint warm water
2 bay leaves, crushed
45g/1½oz desiccated coconut
2 ripe tomatoes, skinned and chopped
2 tbsps freshly chopped coriander leaves (optional)

Clean and wash the channa dahl or the yellow split peas and soak them for at least 2 hours. Drain well. Melt the ghee or butter over a medium heat and fry the onion, cinnamon, cardamoms and red chillies until the onion is lightly browned. Add the dhal, turmeric, chilli powder and salt. Stir-fry for 2-3 minutes, reduce the heat to low and fry the dhal for a further 3-4 minutes, stirring frequently. Add the water, bay leaves, coconut and tomatoes. Bring to the boil, cover the pan and simmer for 35-40 minutes. Stir in the coriander leaves (if using) and season to taste with extra salt if required.

# SABUT MASOOR (WHOLE LENTIL)

*This dhal should be made with whole lentils, either brown or green. I prefer to soak them overnight to give a softer, smoother consistency. Add a little extra water if necessary to give a moist consistency.*

Serves 4

*INGREDIENTS*
60g/2oz butter
1 onion, chopped
1 bay leaf
2.5cm/1 inch cinnamon stick
1 tsp fresh root ginger, peeled and finely grated
2 cloves garlic, peeled and crushed
225g/8oz dhal, washed in 3-4 changes of water
430ml/¾ pint water
1 tsp ground coriander
½ tsp chilli powder
¼ tsp turmeric powder
3 fresh tomatoes, chopped or 3 canned tomatoes, chopped
1 green chilli, chopped
1 tbsp freshly chopped coriander
Salt to taste

Heat the butter and fry the onion until golden brown. Add the bay leaf, cinnamon stick, ginger and garlic and fry for 1 minute. Add the drained dhal and water, cover, bring to the boil and simmer gently for 12-15 minutes. The dhal should be well cooked. Beat it until smooth, then add the ground coriander, chilli and turmeric powder. Stir in the tomatoes, green chilli and fresh coriander. Season with salt and mix well. Cover and cook gently for 7-10 minutes.

Season the dhal with extra salt if necessary. Serve with rice or chapatis and a vegetable curry.

# GREEN LENTILS WITH FRESH GINGER AND SPICES

*This spicy lentil dish is ideal for vegetarians, served with brown rice and a cucumber or vegetable raita.*

Serves 4

*INGREDIENTS*
175g/6oz green or continental
  lentils
Water or stock to cover
30g/1oz ghee or unsalted butter
1 onion, finely chopped
2.5cm/1 inch piece fresh root
  ginger, peeled and grated or
  finely chopped
1 tsp garam masala
1 tsp cumin seeds
1 tsp coriander seeds, crushed
1 tsp green cardamom pods,
  seeds removed and crushed
1 carrot, peeled and diced
400g/14oz can tomatoes
60g/2oz mushrooms, cleaned
  and finely chopped
Salt
1 tbsp cider vinegar
Freshly ground black pepper
Lemon slices
Freshly chopped parsley or
  coriander to garnish

Pick over the lentils and wash
them thoroughly. Place the lentils
in a large, heavy-based saucepan,
cover with water or stock and
bring to the boil. Turn off the
heat, cover and leave the lentils
until they begin to swell.

Meanwhile, heat the ghee or
butter in a separate saucepan
and gently fry the onion, ginger
and spices until they are well
combined, softening and giving
off a tempting aroma. Add the
mixture to the lentils, bring to the
boil and start to add the
remaining vegetables, allowing
several minutes between each
addition, beginning with the
carrot, then the tomatoes and
lastly the chopped mushrooms.
Stir frequently to prevent sticking
and check on the liquid
regularly, adding more water or
stock as necessary.

Just before the end of the
cooking time – approximately 25
minutes depending on the age of
the lentils – add the salt, cider
vinegar and pepper. Cook for a
few more minutes and serve hot,
garnished with slices of lemon
and freshly chopped parsley or
coriander.

# ARHAR TOOR DHAL
# (YELLOW LENTIL)

*This yellow lentil dhal has a thick, smooth consistency and is best served with rice and a chunky vegetable curry, and a selection of chutneys.*

Serves 4

### INGREDIENTS
225g/8oz toor dhal
570ml/1 pint water
¼ tsp turmeric powder
1 tsp ground coriander
¼ tsp salt
6 curry leaves
1 green chilli, split in half
1 tbsp fresh or desiccated coconut
1 tbsp freshly chopped coriander
60g/2oz butter
1 tsp mustard seeds

Wash the toor dhal in 4-5 changes of water then drain. Add the water, turmeric, salt and coriander, cover and simmer gently for 10-15 minutes, until the dhal is well cooked and soft. Beat vigorously until smooth, then add the curry leaves, coconut, chilli and coriander leaves. Cover and cook for a further 8-10 minutes.

Heat the butter and fry the mustard seeds for 30 seconds, then pour them over the dhal. Serve with rice or rotis.

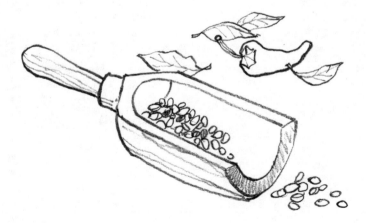

# BESAN LADOO

*Besan is ground chick peas and is generally used as a thickener or a batter ingredient, but in this recipe it is made into a sweetmeat.*

Makes 28-30

*INGREDIENTS*
225g/8oz ghee or unsalted butter
460g/1lb besan, sieved to remove
  the husks
225g/8oz sugar
1½ tsps ground cardamom seeds
60g/2oz chopped mixed nuts

Melt the ghee or butter in a saucepan over medium heat and add the besan. Reduce the heat and fry the besan for 12-15 minutes, stirring continuously. Add the rest of the ingredients, mix thoroughly, then remove the pan from the heat. Allow the mixture to cool completely then form into small walnut-sized balls.

Store in an airtight container. The besan ladoo will remain fresh for 4-5 weeks.

# PLAIN FRIED RICE

*I often think that boiled rice is too plain to serve with curry, yet it is quick and simple to prepare. This recipe for Plain Fried Rice produces a lightly spiced rice requiring the minimum of preparation, which is suitable to·serve with almost any curry.*

Serves 4-6

### INGREDIENTS

275g/10oz basmati or other long-grain rice, washed and soaked in cold water for ½-1 hour
2 tbsps ghee *or* 3 tbsps cooking oil
1 tsp fennel seeds
1 tsp salt
520ml/18 fl oz water for basmati rice *or* 570ml/1 pint for other long-grain rice

Drain the rice and set aside. Heat the oil or ghee over a medium heat and fry the fennel seeds until they are brown. Add the rice and salt, stir and cook for 4-5 minutes, lowering the heat for the last 2-3 minutes of cooking. Add the water to the pan and bring to the boil. Cover and simmer for 12 minutes for basmati rice and 15-18 minutes for long-grain rice without lifting the lid. Leave undisturbed, off the heat, for 10 minutes before serving.

# PILAU RICE

*Pilau rice can be a plain dish or have meat, chicken or fish added to it. It is always fragrant and full of flavours.*

Serves 4-6

*INGREDIENTS*
275g/10oz basmati rice
60g/2oz ghee or unsalted butter
1 large onion, finely sliced
2-4 cloves garlic, peeled and finely chopped
8 whole cloves
8 green cardamoms, the top of each pod split open
2 cinnamon sticks, 5cm/2 inches long, broken up
8 whole peppercorns
1 tsp ground turmeric
570ml/1 pint water
1¼ tsps salt
15g/½ oz butter
30g/1oz seedless sultanas
30g/1oz flaked almonds

Wash the rice and soak in cold water for 30 minutes. Drain well. Melt the ghee or butter in a heavy-based pan over a medium heat and fry the onions until they are soft but not brown. Add the garlic, cloves, cardamoms, cinnamon sticks and peppercorns. Stir and fry until the onions are golden brown, then add the rice and turmeric, and cook for 1-2 minutes. Lower the heat and cook the rice for a further 2-3 minutes. Add the water and the salt, bring to the boil, cover and simmer for 15 minutes without lifting the lid.

Remove the pan from the heat and leave undisturbed for a further 10-12 minutes. Melt the butter over a gentle heat and fry the sultanas until they change colour and swell. Transfer the sultanas to a plate and, in the same fat, fry the almonds until they are lightly browned. Remove to a separate plate. Pile the pilau rice into a warmed serving dish and, using a fork, gently mix in the fried sultanas and almonds.

141

# FRIED BROWN RICE

*I thought this recipe would use brown rice with husks but no!
The rice is almost caramelised in sugar and is quite
delicious. This is the classic accompaniment to dhansak
curries but can be served with any dish.*

Serves 4-6

### INGREDIENTS

275g/10oz basmati or other long-
  grain rice
4 tbsps cooking oil
4 tsps sugar
1 tsp cumin seeds
2 cinnamon sticks, 5cm/2 inches
  long, broken up
6 whole cloves
6 black peppercorns
2 bay leaves, crushed
570ml/1 pint water
1 tsp salt

Wash the rice and soak in cold
water for 30 minutes. Drain well.
Heat the oil over a medium heat
in a heavy-based saucepan and
add the sugar. The sugar will
gradually begin to change colour
to a dark brown. As soon as it
does, add the cumin seeds,
cinnamon, cloves, black
peppercorns and bay leaves. Fry
for 30 seconds, then add the rice
and cook for about 5 minutes,
stirring frequently and lowering
the heat towards the last minute
or two. Add the water and salt.
Bring to the boil, cover and
simmer without lifting the lid.
Cook for 12-15 minutes for
basmati rice, or 15-18 minutes for
long grain rice. Remove the pan
from the heat and leave it
undisturbed for a further 10-15
minutes before serving.

# CARDAMOM RICE

*Cardamoms have a most distinctive flavour – I remember munching them with an Indian friend to clear the taste buds after a very heavy meal. This rice is more subtley flavoured than many pilaus, making it ideal for serving with even the mildest of curries.*

Serves 4-6

### INGREDIENTS

275g/10oz basmati or other long-grain rice
60g/2oz ghee or unsalted butter
6 green cardamoms, the top of each pod split open
1 tsp black cumin seeds or caraway seeds
1 tsp salt
520ml/18 fl oz water for basmati rice *or* 570ml/1 pint for other long-grain rice

Wash the rice, soak in cold water for ½-1 hour and drain thoroughly. Melt the ghee or butter in a large pan over a low heat and fry the cardamoms and caraway seeds for 1 minute. Add the rice, stir and cook over a medium heat for 2-3 minutes then lower the heat and cook for a further 2-3 minutes. Add the salt and water and mix well. Bring to the boil, cover the pan and simmer for 12 minutes for basmati rice and 15-18 minutes for long-grain rice without lifting the lid. Remove from the heat and leave the pan undisturbed for 6-8 minutes.

# BASMATI RICE WITH VEGETABLES

*Basmati is sometimes called 'the Prince of rices' – it certainly
produces the best and most tasty results but only if washed
for some minutes under running water before being cooked
– keep washing until the water runs clear and all the starch
has been removed from the rice.*

Serves 4

### INGREDIENTS

1 red pepper, seeded
1 green pepper, seeded
1 courgette
1 carrot
2 shallots
½ vanilla pod
2 pinches of cinnamon
1 pinch of powdered saffron
½ tsp turmeric
½ tsp curry powder
3 cardamom seeds
3 tbsps oil
340g/12oz basmati rice
1 bouquet garni
570ml/1 pint water
Salt and freshly ground black
    pepper
Fresh coriander

Preheat the oven to
220°C/425°F/Gas Mark 7. Cut the
peppers into evenly-sized strips.
Cut the courgette into chunks,
then slices and finally
matchsticks. Cut the carrot into
slightly smaller matchsticks. Cut
the shallots in half and chop
finely. Slit open the vanilla pod
and run the tip of a knife blade
down the inside to extract the
seeds. Mix the seeds with the
cinnamon, saffron, turmeric,
curry powder and cardamom.

Heat the oil in an ovenproof
casserole and fry the vegetables
for 5 minutes, stirring frequently.
When cooked through, add the
rice and bouquet garni. Continue
frying until the rice becomes
transparent. Add the spices and
some salt and pepper to the
water, then add to the rice and
do not stir again. Cover and cook
in the preheated oven for 25
minutes. When cooked, fluff up
the rice with a fork and serve
garnished with fresh coriander.

# SRI LANKAN RICE

*This is a colourful rice dish, suitable for serving hot with curries or cold as a salad.*

Serves 4

### INGREDIENTS
3 tbsps sunflower oil
1 onion, finely chopped
2 cloves garlic, peeled and crushed
1 tsp ground cumin
1 tsp ground coriander
1 tsp paprika
2 tsps turmeric
¼ tsp chilli powder *or* cayenne pepper
150g/5oz basmati rice, washed and drained
340ml/12 fl oz milk
1 tsp salt
Freshly ground black pepper to taste
225g/8oz mangetout, topped, tailed and cut in half
120g/4oz mushrooms, washed and sliced
150g/5oz sweetcorn
60g/2oz sultanas, washed and soaked

Heat the oil in a large non-stick pan and gently fry the onion and garlic for 4-5 minutes. Add the cumin, coriander, paprika, turmeric and chilli, reduce the heat and fry for a further 3-4 minutes – do not allow the mixture to burn. Add the washed rice, mix well and cook with the onions and spices for about 2 minutes. Add the milk, salt and pepper and stir gently. Bring to the boil, cover and simmer until all the liquid is absorbed and the rice is cooked – approximately 15-20 minutes.

Whilst the rice is cooking, steam the mangetout, mushrooms, sweetcorn and sultanas for 6-8 minutes. Fold the vegetables into the rice after it has stood undisturbed for 10 minutes. Serve hot.

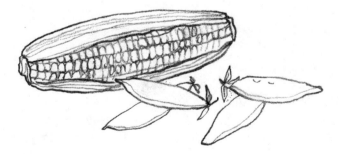

# MIXED VEGETABLE PILAU

*A colourful, well-flavoured pilau that is quick to prepare. I
serve this with Tandoori Chicken or fish. Soak the rice while
you prepare the vegetables.*

Serves 6

*INGREDIENTS*
60g/2oz ghee or unsalted butter
1 large onion, finely sliced
3-4 cloves garlic, peeled and
  finely chopped

*Spices*
1 tsp black cumin seeds or
  caraway seeds
1 tsp coriander seeds
6 black peppercorns
1 bay leaf
2 dried red chillies
1 cinnamon stick, 5cm/2 inches
  long, broken up
6 green cardamoms

½ tsp ground turmeric
225g/8oz cauliflower florets, cut
  into 1.25cm/½ inch pieces
1 small green pepper, seeded
  and cut into 2.5cm/1 inch
  strips
120g/4oz carrots, scraped and
  thinly sliced
275g/10oz basmati rice, washed
  and soaked in cold water for
  30 minutes and drained
60g/2oz frozen garden peas or
  fresh peas boiled until nearly
  tender
60g/2oz frozen sweetcorn
1½ tsp salt
570ml/1 pint water

Melt the ghee or butter in a large
pan over a medium heat and fry
the onions and garlic until
golden brown. Grind the seven
spices in a pestle and mortar and
add with the turmeric. Fry for 2
minutes over a low heat, stirring
frequently, then add the
cauliflower, green pepper and
carrots, stir and cook for 2-3
minutes. Stir in the rice and cook
for a further 2-3 minutes, stirring
constantly. Finally, add the peas,
sweetcorn and salt, and stir well.
Add the water, bring to the boil,
cover the pan and simmer until
the rice has absorbed all the
water for about 12-15 minutes.
Allow about 18 minutes for other
types of long grain rice. Do not
lift the lid or stir the rice during
cooking.

Remove the pan from the heat,
uncover and allow the steam to
escape for 2 minutes. Do not stir
the rice immediately after
cooking. Cover the pan and
leave it undisturbed for 10
minutes before serving.

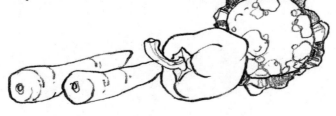

# MATTAR PILAU

*This is a simple pilau rice with peas giving extra colour and flavour – frozen peas are ideal. The rice is coloured yellow with turmeric, a cheaper alternative to saffron.*

Serves 4-6

## INGREDIENTS
275g/10oz basmati rice
90g/3oz ghee or unsalted butter
2 tsps fennel seeds
2-3 dried red chillies
6 whole cloves
2 cinnamon sticks 5cm/2 inches long each, broken up
6 green cardamoms, the top of each pod split open
2 bay leaves, crushed
1 large onion, finely sliced
175g/6oz frozen garden peas
1 tsp ground turmeric
1¼ tsps salt, or to taste
570ml/1 pint water

Wash the rice and soak it in cold water for half an hour. Drain thoroughly. Melt the ghee or butter over a medium heat and fry the fennel seeds until they are brown. Add the chillies, cloves, cinnamon, cardamom and bay leaves. Stir once and add the onions then fry until the onions are lightly browned, stirring frequently. Add the rice, peas, turmeric and salt. Stir and fry for 4-5 minutes, until the rice is fairly dry, lowering the heat for the last 1-2 minutes. Add the water and bring to the boil. Cover the pan and simmer for 12-15 minutes without lifting the lid. Remove the pan from the heat and leave it undisturbed for a further 10-15 minutes. Fork through the rice and serve.

# MUSHROOM PILAU

*Mushrooms and rice blend well to make a tasty pilau. Serve
with a plain vegetable curry or a meat curry of your choice.*

Serves 4-6

*INGREDIENTS*

275g/10oz basmati rice
60g/2oz ghee or unsalted butter
1 tsp caraway seeds
1 large onion, finely sliced
2 cinnamon sticks, each 5cm/2
  inches long, broken up
225g/8oz button mushrooms,
  thickly sliced
½ tsp ground turmeric
1¼ tsps salt
520ml/18 fl oz water
6 green cardamoms, the top of
  each pod split open
6 whole cloves
2 bay leaves, crushed

Wash and soak the rice in cold
water for 30 minutes. Drain and
set aside. Melt the ghee or butter
over a medium heat and fry the
caraway seeds for 30 seconds.
Add the onions and cinnnamon
sticks, and cook until the onions
are golden brown, then add the
rice and fry, stirring constantly,
for 3-4 minutes. Add the
mushrooms, turmeric and salt,
stir and cook for a further 2-3
minutes over a low heat.

Add the water, cardamoms,
cloves and bay leaves to the pan.
Bring to the boil, cover and
simmer for 12-15 minutes. Do
not lift the lid or stir the rice
during cooking. Remove the pan
from the heat, uncover and allow
the steam to escape for 1-2
minutes. Cover the pan and leave
for 10-15 minutes before serving.

# CARROT PILAU

*The younger the carrots, the sweeter the flavour that they will impart to this colourful pilau. Serve with any meat, fish or chicken curry.*

Serves 4-6

### INGREDIENTS

275g/10oz basmati rice, washed and soaked in cold water for ½ hour
520ml/18 fl oz water
1 tsp salt
1 tsp butter or ghee
2 tbsps ghee or unsalted butter
1 tsp cumin or caraway seeds
1 onion, finely sliced
2 cinnamon sticks, each 5cm/2 inches long, broken up
4 green cardamoms, the top of each pod split open
1 tsp garam masala or ground mixed spice
175g/6oz coarsely grated carrots
120g/4oz frozen peas
½ tsp salt

Drain the rice thoroughly and place it in a saucepan with the water. Bring to the boil, then stir in the salt and the teaspoon of butter. Allow the rice to boil steadily for 1 minute, then cover the saucepan and simmer for 12-15 minutes. Do not lift the lid during this time. Remove the pan from heat and keep it covered for a further 10 minutes.

Meanwhile, prepare the rest of the ingredients. Melt the remaining ghee or butter over a medium heat and fry the cumin or caraway seeds until they crackle. Add the onions, cinnamon and cardamom. Fry until the onions are lightly browned, stirring frequently, then add the garam masala or ground mixed spice, stir-fry for 30 seconds. Add the carrots, peas and the salt, stir and cook for 1-2 minutes. Add the cooked rice, stir and mix gently using a metal spoon or a fork, as a wooden spoon or spatula will squash the grains. Remove the pan from the heat and serve.

# NAAN

*I have watched naan breads being cooked, pressed against the sides of a tandoor on special sticks. They will cook well at home in a very hot oven.*

Makes 8 naan

*INGREDIENTS*
460g/1lb plain flour
1 tsp salt
1 tsp kalonji (onion seeds), optional
1 tsp sugar
1½ sachets easy-blend yeast
90ml/3 fl oz milk
150ml/¼ pint natural yogurt
1 medium-sized egg, beaten
60g/2oz ghee or butter
2 tbsps sesame seeds or white poppy seeds

Place the flour, salt, kalonji, sugar and yeast in a large bowl and mix well. Heat the milk until it is lukewarm, reserve 1 tbsp of yogurt and add the rest to the milk and blend thoroughly. Beat the egg and set to one side. Melt the butter or ghee.

Add the milk and yogurt mixture, the egg and ghee or butter to the flour, and knead with your hands or in the food processor or mixer until a soft and springy dough is formed. Place the dough in a large plastic food bag and loosely seal the bag, so that the dough has enough room for expansion.

Leave in a warm place, until doubled in size, in 30-60 minutes. Divide the dough into 8 balls, cover them and set aside for 10-15 minutes.

Preheat the oven to 230°C/450°F/Gas Mark 8 and put an ungreased baking sheet into the oven to preheat for about 10 minutes. Remove the baking sheet from the oven and line it with greased greaseproof paper or baking parchment. Take one of the balls and stretch it gently with both hands to make a teardrop shape. Lay this on the baking sheet and press it gently to stretch it until about 15-17.5cm/6-7 inches in length, maintaining the teardrop shape at all times. Make 2-3 similar shapes at a time and brush with the reserved yogurt, then sprinkle with the sesame or poppy seeds. Bake on the top shelf of the oven for 10-12 minutes, or until puffed and browned. Keep the naan warm in a clean teatowel or foil parcel whilst cooking the remaining breads.

# PARATHAS

*Indian breads are fun to make and very quick to cook as they are generally fried or grilled. We often make our own for a weekend curry. Parathas are rich, with plenty of fat being added following a method almost like that for flaky pastry.*

Makes 4 parathas

## INGREDIENTS

340g/12oz wholemeal flour or chapati flour (atta) plus 1 tbsp extra flour for dusting
½ tsp salt
150g/5oz ghee or unsalted butter
120-150ml/4-5 fl oz warm water

Sift the flour and salt together in a bowl. Rub 60g/2oz of the fat into the flour until thoroughly mixed. Gradually pour in the water, mixing and kneading the mixture to a soft, pliable dough. Divide the dough into 4 equal pieces and flatten them by pressing gently with the palms of your hands.

Dust each flattened portion of dough with the flour and roll out to a circle 20cm/8 inches in diameter. Spread a knob of the remaining fat over each circle of dough. Roll the parathas up into tubes about 2.5cm/1 inch in diameter and 20cm/8 inches long. Gently stretch the dough lengthways and then curl each end inwards in an anti-clockwise direction to resemble a back-to-front letter 'S'. Fold the upper half onto the lower and flatten. Lightly dust all over with flour and roll out the paratha again until the dough is about 20cm/8 inches in diameter and very thin.

Melt the remaining fat and keep to one side. Heat a frying pan (preferably a cast iron one) over a medium heat and place a paratha in it. Turn it over after 30 seconds. Spread 1 tablespoon of the melted fat over the paratha. Flip it over again, lower the heat, and spread 1 tablespoon of the melted fat on the second side of the bread. Press the paratha into the pan with a spatula or palette knife, keeping the dough in contact with the pan. Cook for 1 minute, then turn and cook the second side in the same way. Continue cooking for a few minutes, until the paratha is light brown all over. Wrap in a clean cloth to keep warm whilst cooking the remaining parathas.

# ROTIS

*These are unleavened wholemeal breads. I have made them successfully using a mixture of ordinary brown and white bread flours.*

Makes 8 rotis

Rub the salt and fat into the flour until you reach a rough breadcrumb consistency. Gradually add the water and mix to a soft, pliable dough. Knead lightly then divide the dough into 8. Roll into balls between the palms of your hands, then flatten the balls into round cakes and dust them very lightly with a little plain flour. Roll each into a circle about 15cm/6 inches in diameter; cover the rest of the dough with a damp cloth while you are working on each roti.

Heat a heavy-based frying pan over a medium heat; it is important to have a heavy-based pan as the rotis need even distribution of heat to cook properly. When the pan is hot, place a roti in it and flip it over after about 30 seconds. Spread 1 tsp of ghee or butter over it and turn the roti over. Repeat the process for the other side. Brown both sides evenly and remove from the heat. Line a piece of aluminium foil with absorbent kitchen paper and put the cooked rotis on one end, cover with the other end and seal the edges to make a foil parcel. This will keep the rotis warm for 30-40 minutes.

# CHAPATIS

*These are the best known of all the Indian unleavened breads. They are not too filling, so people may eat two or three, especially if you are not serving rice.*

Makes 14 chapatis

*INGREDIENTS*
340g/12oz fine wholemeal flour
  or atta/chapatti flour
½ tsp salt
15g/1½oz butter or ghee
175ml-280ml/6-10 fl oz warm
  water (the quantity depends on
  the texture of the flour)
1 tbsp extra flour in a shallow
  bowl or plate

Place the flour and salt in a large bowl and rub in the fat. Gradually add the water and keep mixing and kneading until a soft and pliable dough is formed. Cover the dough with a damp cloth and leave in a warm place for 30-60 minutes.

Divide the dough into 14 walnut-sized pieces. Roll each one into a ball, then flatten the ball to make a round cake. Dip each cake into the dry flour and roll the chapati into a circle about 15cm/6 inches in diameter. An iron griddle is normally used for cooking chapatis, but if you do not have one, then use a heavy-based frying pan – the chapaties need even distribution of heat during cooking. Overheating the pan will cause the chapatis to stick and burn.

Heat the griddle or frying pan over a medium heat and place a chapati in it, cook for 30 seconds then turn the chapatti over. Cook until brown spots appear on both sides, turning the chapati over frequently. To keep the chapatis warm, line a piece of aluminium foil with absorbent kitchen paper and place the chapatis on one end, cover with the other end and seal the edges, making a foil parcel. Repeat the cooking method until all the chapatis are cooked – serve hot or warm.

# BATURA

*This unusual bread is made with yogurt which gives it a soft, rich texture. The breads are deep fried after shaping.*

Serves 6

*INGREDIENTS*
340g/12oz plain flour
1 tsp salt
2 tsps easy-blend yeast
1 egg, beaten
150ml/¼ pint natural yogurt
2-3 tbsps warm water
Oil for deep-frying

Place the flour, salt and yeast in a bowl and mix well. Add the egg, yogurt and water and mix until a soft, pliable dough is formed. Alternatively, put all the ingredients in the bowl of a food mixer which has a dough hook, and mix until the dough is formed. Knead the dough lightly and place it in a large plastic food bag. Seal the bag loosely, leaving room for the dough to expand. Leave the dough to rise in a warm place for 3-4 hours, or until doubled in size.

Remove the dough from the bag and divide it into 6 pieces. Shape into balls then flatten into round cakes. Dust lightly with a little flour and roll out into circles about 15cm/6 inches in diameter.

Heat the oil to 180°C; take care not to overheat the oil. Place a batura in the hot oil and fry it for 1 minute; turn it over and fry the other side for a further minute or until it is a rich creamy colour. Drain on absorbent kitchen paper. Roll and fry all the baturas in the same way. It is easier to roll and fry one batura at a time rather than rolling them all out at once.

# LOOCHIS

*Loochis are deep fried puffs of Indian bread, similar to puris. They are made with ordinary white flour and I find them ideal to serve with starters.*

Makes 14-15 loochis

### INGREDIENTS
275g/10oz plain flour plus 1 tbsp extra flour for dusting
½ tsp salt
¼ tsp sugar
1 tsp kalonji (onion seeds), optional
1 tbsp butter, margarine or ghee
150-175ml/5-6 fl oz warm water (this will depend on the texture of the flour)
Oil for deep-frying

In a large bowl, mix together the flour, salt, sugar and kalonji. Rub in the fat and gradually add the water. Either knead with your hands or in the food processor until a stiff dough is formed. Divide the dough into 14-15 walnut-sized pieces. Roll into balls, then press down gently to flatten until about 1.25cm/½ inch thick. When you have shaped all the round cakes, cover them with a damp cloth to prevent them drying out.

Dust each flattened cake lightly with the extra flour and roll out to a circle about 9cm/3½ inches in diameter. It is easier to roll and fry one loochi at a time unless you have someone to help you. Do not stack the rolled loochis on top of each other as they will stick together.

Loochis puff up like balloons during frying. To ensure that the loochis are beautifully puffed, roll them out carefully and evenly without damaging or piercing them. Use a flat perforated spoon for frying.

Heat the oil to 160°C in a deep fryer. Place one loochi at a time in the hot oil – it will soon float to the surface and start puffing up. It helps to cook the loochis evenly if you press them down gently by using the spoon only on the edge of the loochi. As soon as the loochi puffs up, turn it over gently and cook for about 30 seconds or until lightly browned. Drain on absorbent kitchen paper. Fry the rest of the loochis the same way. Keep the fried loochis in a single layer – do not pile one on top of the other as this will damage them.

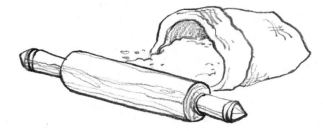

# VEGETABLES

$M$any Indian people, and especially Hindus of higher castes, are vegetarian. The rich variety of vegetables that are grown in India allow for a most inventive and imaginative variety of vegetable dishes within the classic cuisine of the country, a cuisine greatly influenced by religion.

## Mushrooms, a Northern Speciality

Go to any Indian restaurant in the west and you are bound to find several dishes cooked with mushrooms on the menu as well as a mushroom bhaji, a side dish or vegetarian main course. It has therefore been a surprise to discover that mushrooms are certainly not a common vegetable in India, and that they are mainly grown in the north. The Mushroom Bhaji is something of a recent classic, a dish perhaps invented to appeal to the many westerners who now enjoy the rich variety of Indian foods. A classic Indian way of serving mushrooms would be in a curry as a starter, allowing the mushrooms to be savoured for their own flavour.

## Spinach – my Favourite Vegetable for Indian Cooking

There are many vegetables without which you simply cannot begin to make a good curry – onions and chillies immediately spring to mind but, for me, one of the most versatile of vegetables is spinach. In the west we have the advantage of being able to purchase spinach chopped and frozen – so convenient for a side dish to be cooked in a hurry. Saag is the Indian term for spinach and Saag Bhaji is one of my favourite side dishes – I sometimes add a little desiccated coconut if I serve it with a chicken curry as I find the flavours all blend well together. However, if you are cooking for a vegetarian, I thoroughly recommend the recipe for Palak Paneer (Paneer and Spinach) – paneer is a simple Indian cheese and adds plenty of protein to a vegetarian meal.

## Know Your Chillies – an Essential Indian Ingredient

So many Indian recipes call for chillies. When used fresh they are usually green and very hot – Indian chillies are long and thin; the fat, squat chillies available in supermarkets are milder and are more commonly associated with African cookery. As with all peppers, the chillies turn red as they ripen and become slightly less fiery in flavour and a little sweeter. The Indians, however, tend to use red chillies dried and this concentrates the flavour and the heat of the vegetable.

The hottest parts of the chilli are the seeds around the core. Many Indians will cook with these to add extra fire to the dish but the seeds may be removed if a milder flavour is preferred. Cut the chillies in half lengthways and scrape out the seeds. Chop the chilli flesh very finely and remember to wash your hands very thoroughly immediately after dealing with the chillies – rubbing my eyes with chilli fingers is one of the most painful experiences I have ever had in the kitchen.

If you are just beginning to experiment with Indian cookery you should go easy with the chillies. An old hand at Indian dishes will have built up a tolerance to the heat and may well like to add three or four chillies to a dish, whereas one or a maximum of two will be sufficient for the novice. Chillies, either as a vegetable or dried and ground as a spice, contribute the heat to Indian food. When cooking for friends it is advisable to err on the side of caution with the chillies – many people find it embarrassing if the curry is too hot for them to enjoy. Incidentally, milk is far more soothing than water if the curry is too hot!

## Potatoes – Vegetable or Snack Food?

Potatoes are one of the most successful vegetables for including in side dishes or for serving as a vegetable main course. They absorb flavours well and are delicious when cooked simply with fresh spices, for example fenugreek or coriander leaves. They also combine well with other root vegetables to provide substantial vegetable main courses and Gobi Aloo, a lightly spiced dish of cauliflower and potatoes originating in northern India, must surely be one of the best-known and most popular of vegetable combinations. However, I usually think of sweet potatoes when considering Indian vegetable dishes and it is interesting to note that, because of their sweet fragrant flavour (very similar to that of a parsnip), sweet potatoes are usually lightly fried and served as a savoury snack rather than as part of a meal.

# MIXED VEGETABLE CURRY

*I often find that my vegetable curries have a tendency to taste the same! Here green chillies are added towards the end of cooking for extra flavour and colour.*

Serves 4-6

### INGREDIENTS

4-5 tbsps cooking oil
1 large onion, finely chopped
1.25cm/½ inch piece of fresh root ginger, peeled and finely sliced
1 tsp ground turmeric
1 tsp ground coriander
1 tsp ground cumin
1 tsp paprika
4 small ripe tomatoes, skinned and chopped *or* a 200g/7oz can of tomatoes with their juice
225g/8oz potatoes, peeled and diced
90g/3oz French or dwarf beans, sliced
120g/4oz carrots, scraped and sliced
90g/3oz garden peas, shelled weight
430ml/¾ pint warm water
2-4 whole fresh green chillies
1 tsp garam masala
1 tsp salt
1 tbsp freshly chopped coriander leaves

Heat the oil over a medium heat and fry the onions until they are lightly browned. Add the ginger and fry for a further 30 seconds, then reduce the heat and add the turmeric, coriander, cumin and paprika. Stir well. Add half the tomatoes and fry for 2 minutes, stirring continuously, then add all the other vegetables and the water. Mix well and bring to the boil, then cover and simmer until vegetables are tender, for about 15-20 minutes.

Add the remaining tomatoes and the green chillies to the curry. Cover and simmer for 5-6 minutes, then add the garam masala and salt, and mix well. Stir in half the coriander leaves and remove the pan from the heat. Place the vegetable curry in a warmed serving dish and scatter the remaining coriander leaves over the top.

# CAULIFLOWER MASALA

*Cauliflower Masala is a well-flavoured vegetable curry which is suitable for serving either as a main dish or as a vegetable accompaniment.*

Serves 4-6

## INGREDIENTS

1 cauliflower
2 potatoes
4 tbsps cooking oil
1 tsp cumin seeds
1 large onion, finely sliced
½ tsp ground turmeric
1 tsp ground coriander
1 tsp ground cumin
¼-½ tsp chilli powder
2 ripe tomatoes, skinned and
    chopped
175ml/6 fl oz warm water
120g/4oz shelled peas, fresh or
    frozen (cook fresh peas until
    they are tender before using)
1-2 fresh green chillies, seeded
    and slit lengthways into halves
1 tsp salt
½ tsp garam masala
1 tbsp freshly chopped coriander
    leaves

Cut the cauliflower into 1.25cm/½ inch florets – wash and drain. Peel and cut the potatoes lengthways into 12.5cm/½ inch thick strips.

Heat the oil over a medium heat and add the cumin seeds. As soon as they start to pop, add the onions and fry until they are soft. Reduce the heat to low and add the turmeric, coriander, cumin and chilli powder. Stir and fry for 2-3 minutes then add the chopped tomatoes. Fry for a further 2-3 minutes, stirring continuously. Add the potatoes and the water. Bring to the boil, cover the pan and simmer for 6-8 minutes, until the potatoes are half-cooked. Add the cauliflower, cover the pan again and simmer for about 10 minutes, until the potatoes are tender.

Stir in the peas, green chillies, salt and garam masala. Cover the pan and cook for a further 5 minutes. Remove from the heat and stir in the coriander leaves, then serve immediately.

# KHUMBI AUR BESAN KI BHAJI (MUSHROOMS WITH GRAM FLOUR)

*Mushrooms are not all that common in India, but there are a few glorious mushroom dishes that are amongst my personal favourites. I always find that mushrooms provide a good colour contrast in an Indian meal.*

Serves 4

### INGREDIENTS
340g/12oz white mushrooms
2 tbsps cooking oil
2-3 cloves garlic, peeled and crushed
½ tsp salt
½ tsp chilli powder
2 tbsps freshly chopped coriander leaves
1 tbsp lemon juice
2 tbsps besan (gram flour or chick pea flour), sieved

Wash the mushrooms and chop them roughly.

Heat the oil over a medium heat and add the garlic. Allow it to brown slightly, then add the mushrooms. Stir and cook for 2 minutes. Add the salt, chilli powder and coriander leaves, and cook for 1 minute, then add the lemon juice and mix well. Sprinkle the besan over the mushroom mixture, and stir to mix immediately. Add extra salt if necessary and serve.

# CABBAGE WITH CINNAMON

*A most unusual combination of ingredients producing a delicious, mildly spiced side dish. A handful of frozen peas may be added for extra colour.*

Serves 4-6

### INGREDIENTS
4 tbsps cooking oil
1 large onion, finely sliced
2 fresh green chillies, sliced lengthways; seeds removed if a milder flavour is preferred
3 cinnamon sticks, 5cm/2 inches long, broken up into 2-3 pieces
1 large potato, peeled and cut into 2.5cm/1 inch dice
½ tsp ground turmeric
¼ tsp chilli powder
120ml/4 fl oz warm water
1 small white cabbage, finely shredded
1 tsp salt
1 tbsp freshly chopped coriander leaves

Heat the oil over a medium heat and fry the onions, green chillies and cinnamon sticks until the onions are soft. Add the potatoes, and fry over a low heat for 6-8 minutes. Stir in the turmeric and chilli powder, and add the water. Bring it to the boil, cover the pan and simmer for 6-8 minutes, until the potatoes are half cooked. Add the cabbage and salt, and mix well. Reduce the heat to the minimum setting, cover the pan and cook until the vegetables are tender (the cabbage should not be mushy). The finished dish should be fairly moist but not wet. If there is too much liquid left in the pan, remove the lid and let the liquid evaporate. Stir in the coriander leaves, add extra salt if necessary and serve.

# POTATOES WITH POPPY SEEDS

*Poppy seeds do not only provide texture to dishes – they also add a delicate but distinctive flavour.*

Serves 4-6

## INGREDIENTS
5 tbsps cooking oil
½ tsp kalonji (onion seeds), optional
1 tsp cumin seeds
4-6 cloves garlic, peeled and crushed
1 tsp freshly ground black pepper
½ tsp ground turmeric
680g/1½lbs potatoes, peeled and diced
1 fresh green chilli, finely chopped
6 tbsps white poppy seeds
1 tsp salt

Heat the oil to smoking point in a non-stick or cast iron pan. Remove the pan from the heat and add the kalonji (if using) and cumin seeds. As soon as the seeds start crackling, add the garlic and return the pan to a medium heat. Add the ground black pepper and turmeric, stir briskly then add the potatoes and green chilli. Fry for 2-3 minutes, stirring constantly. Reduce the heat to low, cover the pan and cook for 12-15 minutes, until the potatoes are tender, stirring occasionally.

Meanwhile, roughly grind the poppy seeds in a pestle and mortar or coffee grinder. Add to the potatoes, increase the heat to medium and fry the potato and poppy seed mixture for 5-6 minutes, stirring frequently. Stir in the salt and serve immediately.

# GREEN BEANS IN GARLIC BUTTER

*This is a winning combination of ingredients and the dish is bound to be popular with everyone.*

Serves 4-6

### INGREDIENTS
30g/1oz unsalted butter
½ tsp cumin seeds
3-4 cloves garlic, peeled and crushed or finely chopped
¼-½ tsp chilli powder
460g/1lb whole green beans, fresh or frozen
½ tsp salt

Melt the butter over a low heat and fry the cumin seeds for 30 seconds. Add the garlic and fry for 1 minute, then add the chilli powder and the beans. Stir and fry for 1-2 minutes. Add the salt and mix thoroughly. Cover the pan and simmer the beans for 10-12 minutes in their own juice until they are tender, stirring occasionally. Serve immediately.

# CAULIFLOWER WITH MUSTARD SEED

*I often serve cauliflower with a mustard sauce – this cauliflower side dish is spiced with mustard seeds.*

Serves 4-6

### INGREDIENTS

1 large cauliflower
6 tbsps vegetable oil
1 tbsp whole black mustard
   seeds
2 tsps whole fennel seeds
1 tsp whole cumin seeds
¼ tsp turmeric
4 cloves garlic, peeled and finely
   chopped
1 tsp salt
2 fresh green chillies, finely
   chopped
Cold water

Cut the cauliflower into small florets, then wash and drain them. Heat the oil in a large, heavy-based frying pan over a medium heat. When hot, add the mustard, fennel and cumin seeds. Once the mustard seeds start to pop add the turmeric, garlic, salt and chilli and stir-fry until lightly browned. Add a few tablespoons of water and the cauliflower and cook for about 5 minutes, until the cauliflower is cooked but still firm. Add extra water if necessary. Serve immediately.

# ALOO GAJJAR
# (POTATO AND CARROTS)

*Potatoes and carrots make a good base for a vegetable curry
and the flavour of the carrots is accentuated by adding a
little lemon juice to the vegetables just before serving.*

Serves 2-3

### INGREDIENTS
60g/2oz ghee or
2 tbsps oil
1 tsp cumin seeds
2 potatoes, peeled and cut into
    1.25cm/½ inch dice
3 carrots, peeled and diced
1 tsp chilli powder
1 tsp ground coriander
¼ tsp turmeric powder
Salt to taste
Juice of ½ lemon

Heat the ghee or oil in a large frying pan and add the cumin seeds. When they start to pop, add the potatoes. Fry for 3-4 minutes, then add the carrots. Stir in the chilli, coriander, turmeric powder and salt. Stir fry the mixture for 1-2 minutes then cover and cook on a low heat for 8-10 minutes. Add just a little water to help cook the carrots. Pour the lemon juice over just before serving.

# SAAG (SPINACH) BHAJI

*This is my very favourite side dish – I use fresh spinach from the garden or frozen chopped spinach.*

Serves 4-6

### INGREDIENTS
6 tbsps cooking oil
½ tsp black mustard seeds
1 tsp cumin seeds
8-10 fenugreek seeds (optional)
1 tbsp curry leaves
2-3 cloves garlic, peeled and finely chopped
2-4 dried red chillies, roughly chopped
460g/1lb fresh leaf spinach *or* 225g/8oz frozen leaf spinach, finely chopped
15g/½oz ghee or unsalted butter
1 large potato, peeled and diced
1 large onion, finely sliced
½ tsp ground turmeric
1 tsp ground cumin
½ tsp garam masala
¼-½ tsp chilli powder
2-3 ripe tomatoes, skinned and chopped
1 tsp salt

Heat 2 tbsps of oil over a medium heat and fry the mustard seeds until they pop. Add the cumin seeds, fenugreek (if using) and curry leaves with the garlic and red chillies. Allow the garlic to brown slightly. Add the spinach, and mix thoroughly. Cover and simmer for 15 minutes, stirring occasionally.

Melt the ghee or butter in a frying pan over a medium heat and brown the diced potatoes. Remove from the heat and set to one side.

Heat the remaining oil over a medium heat and fry the onions until well browned, taking care not to burn the onions or they will taste bitter. Reduce the heat to minimum and add the turmeric, cumin, garam masala and chilli powder, stir and fry for 2-3 minutes. Add the spinach, potatoes, tomatoes and salt, cover and simmer for 10 minutes or until the potatoes are tender, stirring occasionally. Remove from heat, add extra salt if necessary and serve.

# BUTTER BEANS AND GREEN PEPPER

*Butter beans and green pepper combine to give a most unusual, light, buttery flavour to this dish. It is dry, with next to no sauce, so is ideal for serving as a side dish with a curry that has plenty of sauce.*

Serves 4

### INGREDIENTS
1 tbsp oil
1 onion, chopped
225g/8oz butter beans or broad
  beans
1 large green pepper, seeded and
  chopped
¼ tsp turmeric
½ tsp chilli powder
1 tsp ground coriander
Salt
4-5 fresh or canned tomatoes,
  chopped
1 green chilli, chopped
1 tbsp freshly chopped coriander
  leaves

Heat the oil and fry the onion for 3-4 minutes. Add the beans and green pepper, and cook for 4-5 minutes. Stir in the turmeric, chilli and ground coriander and add salt to taste and the tomatoes. Mix well. Cover and cook for 5-6 minutes over a low heat, then add the green chilli and fresh coriander. Cook covered for 2-3 minutes. If the mixture is too dry, add 2 tbsps water.

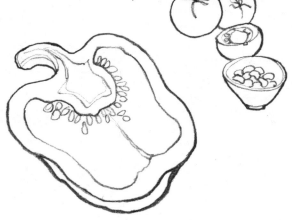

# STUFFED PEPPERS

*Stuffed peppers are an unusual Indian side dish, colourful and delicious.*

Serves 6-8

*INGREDIENTS*
60g/2oz ghee *or* 3 tbsps oil
1 onion, finely chopped
1 potato, peeled and diced
225g/8oz mixed frozen
  vegetables
1 tsp garam masala
½ tsp chilli powder
2 tsp dried mango powder
Salt
6-8 small green peppers
Oil for frying

Preheat the oven to 160°C/325°F/Gas Mark 3. Heat the ghee or oil and fry the onion until tender. Add the potatoes and cook for 4-5 minutes, then add the mixed vegetables, and garam masala, chilli powder, mango powder and salt to taste. Cover and cook gently until potatoes are tender, then remove from the heat and cool.

Wash and dry the green peppers. Remove the tops by slicing across to form a lid. Remove the pith and seeds. Heat 3 tbsps of oil in a frying pan and fry the peppers laid sideways, for 1-2 minutes, cooking them on all sides. Drain well. Stuff each pepper with filling and place on a baking tray. Bake in the preheated oven for 20 minutes, then serve.

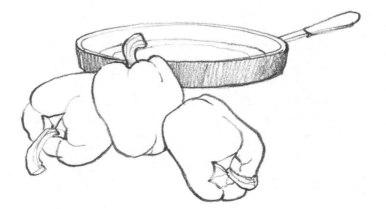

# BHAREY BHINDI (WHOLE STUFFED OKRA)

*The okra are really spiced, not stuffed, and served with a tasty onion dressing.*

Serves 4-6

### INGREDIENTS

225g/8oz bhindi (okra), washed, dried, topped and tailed
90g/3oz ghee *or* 4 tbsps oil
1 large onion, thickly sliced
2 tsp ground coriander
2 tsp ground cumin
1 tsp turmeric powder
1 tsp chilli powder
Salt
1 tbsp dry mango powder
1 tbsp aniseed (sauf) powder

Split the okra or bhindi halfway down. Melt 30g/1oz of ghee or 1 tbsp oil in a pan over a medium heat, add the onion and cook for 30 seconds. Set to one side. Mix the coriander, cumin, turmeric and chilli powder, and put a little of this spice mixture into the split okras. Heat the remaining ghee or oil in a frying pan or wok, add the stuffed okras. Sprinkle with salt and stir well. Cover and cook slowly for 5-6 minutes, then add the fried onions, and sprinkle with the mango and aniseed powder. Cover and cook for 3-4 minutes.

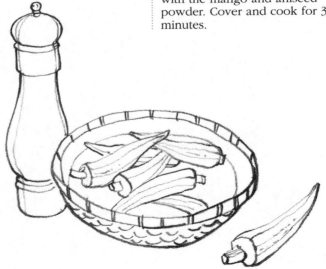

# TENDLI BHAJI WITH CASHEW NUTS

*Tendli is an Asian vegetable which tastes like courgettes but looks like a gooseberry. Use courgettes if tendli is not available.*

Serves 4

### INGREDIENTS
2 tbsps oil
60g/2oz cashew nuts
3-4 cloves of garlic, peeled and crushed
½ tsp mustard seeds
6-8 curry leaves
2-3 dry red chillies or fresh green chillies
225g/8oz tendli, washed, dried and cut in half lengthways
Salt
2 tsps desiccated coconut
¼ tsp turmeric powder

Heat the oil and fry the cashew nuts until lightly browned. Remove with a slotted spoon, then fry the garlic until lightly browned in the same oil. Add the mustard seeds, curry leaves and red or green chillies and fry for 30 seconds. Add the tendli, sprinkle with salt and stir. Add the desiccated coconut, turmeric and fried cashew nuts, cover and cook slowly for 10-12 minutes, or until the tendli is tender.

# VEGETABLE NIRAMISH

*This mixed vegetable curry is ideal for vegetarians, or for serving as a side dish with a meat or chicken curry. Use a selection of fresh vegetables in season.*

Serves 4

### INGREDIENTS
1 small aubergine
Salt
3 tbsps vegetable oil
1 onion, sliced
1 green chilli, seeded and finely chopped
1 tsp cumin seeds
1 large potato, peeled and cut into chunks
120g/4oz cauliflower florets
1 small green pepper, seeded and sliced
2 small carrots, peeled and thickly sliced
1 tsp ground coriander
1 tsp turmeric
1 tsp chilli powder
150ml/¼ pint vegetable stock
1 tsp freshly chopped coriander
Juice of 1 lime
Fresh chillies to garnish

Cut the aubergine into chunks and sprinkle liberally with salt, then allow to stand for 30 minutes. Rinse well and drain. Heat the oil in a saucepan and fry the onion, green chilli and cumin seeds for 2 minutes, then stir in the potato and fry for 3 minutes. Add the aubergine, cauliflower, pepper and carrots and fry for a further 3 minutes. Stir in the spices and fry for 1 minute, then add the stock. Cover and simmer gently for 30 minutes until all the vegetables are tender, adding a little more stock if necessary. Add the coriander and lime juice and simmer for 2 minutes. Serve garnished with fresh chillies.

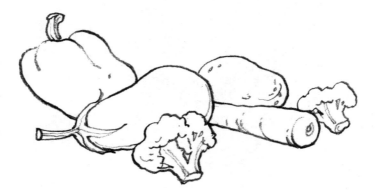

# EGG & POTATO DUM

*I love curried eggs and find them a wonderful dish to
prepare when time and money are short.*

Serves 4-6

### INGREDIENTS

6 hard-boiled eggs
5 tbsps cooking oil
460g/1lb potatoes, peeled and
  quartered
Pinch of turmeric
Pinch of chilli powder
1 large onion, finely chopped
1.25cm/½ inch piece of fresh
  root ginger, peeled and grated
1 cinnamon stick, 5cm/2 inches
  long, broken into 2-3 pieces
2 brown cardamoms, the top of
  each pod split open
4 whole cloves
1 fresh green chilli, chopped
200g/7oz can tomatoes
½ tsp ground turmeric
2 tsps ground coriander
1 tsp ground fennel
¼-½ tsp chilli powder (optional)
1 tsp salt
225ml/8 fl oz warm water
1 tbsp freshly chopped coriander
  leaves

Shell the eggs and make 4 slits
lengthways through each egg
white, taking care not to cut right
• to the top or the bottom. Heat
the oil in a cast iron or non-stick
pan over medium heat (enamel
or steel pans will cause the eggs
and the potatoes to stick) Fry the
potatoes until they are well
browned on all sides, then
remove them with a slotted
spoon and set to one side.
Remove the pan from the heat
and stir in the turmeric and chilli.
Return the pan to the heat and
fry the whole eggs until they are
well browned. Remove them
with a slotted spoon and set to
one side. Fry the onions, ginger,
cinnamon, cardamom, cloves and
green chilli in the same oil, until
the onions are lightly browned.
Add half the tomatoes, and cook
until the tomatoes break up, then
add the turmeric, ground
coriander, fennel and chilli
powder (if using); stir and cook
for 3-4 minutes. Add the rest of
the tomatoes and cook for 4-5
minutes, stirring frequently.
Return the potatoes to the pan
with the salt and water. Bring to
the boil, cover the pan tightly
and simmer until the potatoes are
tender, stirring occasionally. Add
the eggs and simmer, uncovered
for 5-6 minutes, stirring once or
twice. Stir in the coriander
leaves, and serve.

# MUSHROOM BHAJI

*Anyone who visits Indian restaurants might think that mushrooms are a popular Indian ingredient but this is not so! Mushroom Bhaji, one of the most popular of vegetable side dishes, has really been developed for the Western restaurant trade!*

Serves 4

*INGREDIENTS*

3-4 tbsps cooking oil
1 onion, finely chopped
2-3 cloves garlic, peeled and
   crushed
½ tsp ground turmeric
½ tsp chilli powder
1 tsp ground coriander
1 tsp ground cumin
¾ tsp salt
1 tbsp tomato purée
225g/8oz mushrooms, chopped

Heat the oil over medium heat and fry the onions until they are lightly browned. Lower the heat and add the garlic, turmeric, chilli powder, coriander and cumin. Stir and fry the spices, adding about 1 tbsp of water to prevent the spices from sticking to the bottom of the pan. As soon as this water dries up, add a little more. Continue doing this until you have fried the spices for about 5 minutes.

Add the salt and tomato purée to the pan, then add the mushrooms. Stir until thoroughly mixed, then add about 2 tbsps of water and cover the pan. Simmer for 10 minutes. The finished dish should have a small amount of gravy but it should not be too wet. Reduce any excess liquid by fast boiling before serving the bhaji.

# AUBERGINE BHARTA

*A bharta is a dish of puréed or mashed vegetables, spiced for extra flavour.*

Serves 4

### INGREDIENTS

1 large aubergine weighing about 460g/1lb
4 tbsps cooking oil
½ tsp black mustard seeds
½ tsp fennel seeds
2.5cm/1 inch piece of fresh root ginger, peeled and grated
2-3 cloves garlic, peeled and crushed
1 fresh green chilli, finely chopped
1 large onion, finely chopped
½ tsp ground turmeric
¼-½ tsp chilli powder (optional)
2 small ripe tomatoes, skinned and chopped
1 tsp salt
15g/½oz freshly chopped coriander leaves
1 small tomato, sliced

Wash the aubergine and make 2-3 small incisions in it. This is to prevent the aubergine from bursting during cooking. Preheat the grill to medium and cook the aubergine for 12-15 minutes or until tender. Turn it frequently during cooking. Remove the aubergine and allow it to cool. Cut the aubergine lengthways into two. Scrape out the flesh with a knife or spoon and discard the skin. Purée the flesh in a food processor or mash it with a fork.

Heat the oil over a medium heat and add the mustard seeds; as soon as they begin to pop add the fennel seeds, ginger, garlic and green chilli. Stir and fry the ingredients for 1 minute then add the onions. Fry the onions until they are just soft, then stir in the turmeric and chilli powder. Add the tomatoes and cook for 2 minutes, then stir in the aubergine and salt, and cook for 2-3 minutes. Add half the coriander leaves and remove the pan from heat. Place the aubergine bharta in a warmed serving dish and garnish with the sliced tomato. Scatter the remaining coriander leaves on top.

# BHINDI (OKRA) MASALA

*I love okra – they have a delicate yet distinctive flavour which is enhanced by light or medium spicing. Try to choose small, evenly-sized okra for this recipe.*

Serves 4

### INGREDIENTS
225g/8oz bhindi (okra)
2 tbsps cooking oil
1 tsp ground coriander
¼ tsp ground cumin
½ tsp garam masala
¼ tsp ground turmeric
200g/7oz can tomatoes
¼ tsp chilli powder
½ tsp salt
1 tbsp freshly chopped coriander
  leaves

Scrub each bhindi gently, wash them and slice off the tops. Heat the oil over a medium heat in a wide shallow pan. When hot, remove the pan from the heat and add the ground coriander, cumin, garam masala and turmeric. The pan is removed from the heat so as not to burn the spices. Return the pan to the heat and add the tomatoes and the chilli powder. Stir and cook for 2-3 minutes, then add the whole bhindis and the salt. Stir and cover the pan. Lower the heat to the minimum setting and cook for about 10 minutes. Stir once or twice during this time. When cooked, the bhindi should be tender but still firm. Place the bhindi in a warmed serving dish and scatter the coriander leaves on top.

# CABBAGE WITH GRAM FLOUR

*Cabbage, fresh spinach or kale may all be used with equal success in this quickly prepared dish.*

Serves 4-6

### INGREDIENTS
4 tbsps cooking oil
½ tsp black mustard seeds
½ tsp cumin seeds
8-10 fenugreek seeds
3-4 cloves garlic, peeled and crushed
Pinch of asaphoetida (optional)
1 onion, finely shredded
¼ tsp ground turmeric
½ tsp chilli powder
275-340g/10-12oz white cabbage, finely shredded
1 tsp salt
60ml/2 fl oz water
2 tbsps besan (gram flour or chick pea flour), sieved

Heat the oil in a wide shallow pan over a medium heat and fry the mustard seeds until they pop. Add the cumin seeds and the fenugreek, then stir in the garlic and allow it to brown slightly. Add the asaphoetida (if using) and the onions, turmeric and chilli powder. Stir and fry for 1-2 minutes, then add the cabbage and salt, and mix thoroughly. Reduce the heat to low, cover the pan and cook for 8-10 minutes, stirring occasionally. The cabbage should be cooked but still slightly crisp. Sprinkle the water evenly on the cabbage, then the besan and cook for 1-2 minutes stirring continuously. Serve immediately.

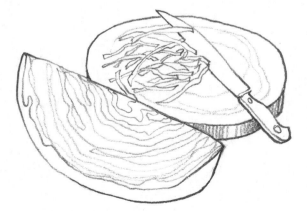

# ALOO MATTAR
# (POTATOES AND PEAS)

*Potatoes are often used as the main ingredient for side dishes and are served in the same way as any other vegetable – with rice or breads.*

Serves 4-6

### INGREDIENTS
4 tbsps cooking oil
1 onion, finely chopped
2 cinnamon sticks, 5cm/2 inches long, broken up
1.25cm/½ inch piece of fresh root ginger, peeled and finely chopped
½ tsp ground turmeric
2 tsps ground cumin
¼ tsp chilli powder
¼ tsp freshly ground black pepper
460g/1lb potatoes, peeled and cut into 2.5cm/1 inch cubes
1-2 whole fresh green chillies
1 tbsp tomato purée
1 tsp salt
225ml/8 fl oz warm water
120g/4oz frozen peas
1 tbsp freshly chopped coriander leaves (optional)

Heat the oil over a medium heat and fry the onion, cinnamon and ginger for 4-5 minutes, stirring frequently. Reduce the heat to low and add the turmeric, cumin, chilli powder and black pepper. Stir and fry for 1 minute, then add the potatoes and green chillies, and cook for 2-3 minutes until the spices are thoroughly blended. Stir in the tomato purée and salt, then add the water. Bring to the boil, cover the pan and cook over a medium to low heat for 10 minutes, until the potatoes are half cooked. Add the peas, cover the pan and cook until the potatoes are tender. Remove the pan from the heat, stir in half the coriander leaves and scatter the remainder on top.

178

# BHINDI (OKRA) WITH COCONUT

*Many people find the texture of okra to be a little too smooth – the poppy and sesame seeds in this recipe add extra texture, even after they have been ground.*

Serves 4

### INGREDIENTS
225g/8oz bhindi (okra)
2 tbsps sesame seeds
1 tbsp white poppy seeds
2 tbsps desiccated coconut
1-2 dried red chillies
1 fresh green chilli, roughly chopped
3 tbsps cooking oil
½ tsp black mustard seeds
¼ tsp fenugreek seeds
2 cloves garlic, peeled and finely chopped or crushed
½ tsp salt

Wash the bhindi, trim off the stalks and cut each bhindi into two pieces. Heat an iron griddle or heavy-based pan over a medium heat and dry-roast the sesame and poppy seeds until they are lightly browned. Transfer the seeds to a plate and allow them to cool. Reheat the griddle and dry-roast the coconut until lightly browned, stirring constantly. Transfer the coconut to a plate and allow it to cool.

Roughly grind the sesame and poppy seeds, and the dried red chillies in a coffee grinder or pestle and mortar. Add the coconut and fresh green chilli and grind until smooth. Heat the oil over a medium heat and add the mustard seeds. As soon as the seeds start to pop, add the fenugreek and garlic. Allow the garlic to brown slightly then add the bhindi and salt; stir and mix thoroughly. Lower the heat to the minimum setting, cover the pan and cook for about 10 minutes, stirring occasionally. Stir in the ground ingredients and mix well. Remove from the heat, add extra salt if necessary and serve immediately.

# SPICED GREEN BEANS

*Green beans make wonderful Indian side dishes – as the runner bean season progresses you will welcome this recipe for using up your surplus produce.*

Serves 4-6

*INGREDIENTS*
2 tbsps sesame seeds
3 tbsps cooking oil
¼ tsp black mustard seeds
4-6 cloves garlic, peeled and
    finely chopped
1-2 dried red chillies, roughly
    chopped
½ tsp ground turmeric
1 tsp ground coriander
460g/1lb frozen sliced green
    beans, defrosted and drained,
    or fresh in season
¾ tsp salt
1 tbsp desiccated coconut

Heat an iron griddle or heavy-based pan over a medium heat and dry-roast the sesame seeds until they are lightly browned, stirring constantly. Transfer them to a plate and allow to cool. Heat the oil in a pan over a medium heat and add the mustard seeds. When they begin to pop, add the garlic and allow it to brown slightly, then add the red chillies, turmeric and coriander, stir briskly and add the beans and salt. Mix thoroughly, reduce the heat to the minimum setting, cover the pan tightly and cook until the beans are tender, stirring occasionally. This will take 15-20 minutes. Grind the sesame seeds and the coconut in a pestle and mortar or a coffee grinder and stir them into the beans. Season with extra salt if necessary and serve.

# KASHMIRI DUM ALOO (SPICED POTATOES WITH YOGURT)

*New potatoes are fried until brown and then dressed with yogurt and spices in this delicious vegetable dish. The green chilli is added as a garnish at the end of cooking, providing a fiery garnish.*

Serves 4

### INGREDIENTS

570g/1¼lbs small new potatoes
30g/1oz ghee or unsalted butter
1 tsp fennel seeds

*Ground spices*
½ tsp ground cumin
1 tsp ground coriander
¼ tsp freshly ground black
  pepper
½ tsp ground turmeric
½ tsp ground ginger

150g/5oz thick-set natural yogurt
1 tsp salt
¼ tsp garam masala
1 tbsp freshly chopped coriander
  leaves
1 fresh green chilli, seeded and
  finely chopped

Boil the potatoes in their skins, allow them to cool then peel. Prick the potatoes all over with a cocktail stick to enable the spices to penetrate deep inside. Melt the ghee over a medium heat in a non-stick or cast iron pan (steel or enamel pans will cause the potatoes to stick and break up). When the ghee is hot, fry the potatoes in a single layer until they are well browned, turning them over frequently. Remove them with a slotted spoon and set aside.

Remove the pan from the heat and stir in the fennel seeds and the ground spice mixture. Adjust the heat to low and place the pan back on the heat, stir the spices and fry for 1 minute. Add the yogurt and salt, and mix well, then add the potatoes, cover the pan and simmer for 10-12 minutes. Add the garam masala and remove the pan from the heat. Stir in the coriander leaves and the green chilli and serve.

# FRENCH BEAN AND POTATO BHAJI

*French beans and potatoes – two of my favourite side dish vegetables combined in a wonderfully flavoured bhaji*

Serves 4-6

*INGREDIENTS*
4-5 tbsps cooking oil
½ tsp black mustard seeds
½ tsp cumin seeds
1 large onion, finely sliced
3-4 dried red chillies, roughly
    chopped
10-12 fenugreek seeds
15g/½oz freshly chopped
    coriander leaves,
½ tsp ground turmeric
1 large potato, peeled and cut
    into matchsticks
275g/10oz French beans, sliced
1 tsp salt
1 tsp ground cumin

Heat the oil over a medium heat and add the mustard seeds. As soon as the seeds start to pop, add the cumin seeds, onions, red chillies and fenugreek. Fry for 3-4 minutes, stirring frequently. Add the coriander leaves and turmeric, and fry for 1 minute, then add the potatoes, beans and salt. Stir until the ingredients are thoroughly mixed, then cover the pan and cook on the lowest setting for about 25 minutes, until the vegetables are tender, stirring occasionally. Add the ground cumin, cook for a further 2-3 minutes then serve.

# POTATOES WITH GARLIC AND CHILLIES

*A spicy shallow-fried Indian chip – perfect for serving with plainly cooked meat or fish.*

Serves 4-6

### INGREDIENTS
460g/1lb potatoes, peeled
3 tbsps cooking oil
½ tsp black mustard seeds
½ tsp cumin seeds
4 cloves garlic, peeled and crushed
¼-½ tsp chilli powder
½ tsp ground turmeric
1 tsp salt

Cut the potatoes to the thickness of short French fries. Heat the oil over a medium heat in a wide, shallow non-stick or cast iron pan. Add the mustard seeds and cumin. When the seeds start popping, add the garlic and allow it to brown lightly. Remove the pan from the heat and add the chilli powder and turmeric, then add the potatoes and return the pan to the heat. Stir and increase the heat to medium. Add the salt, stir and cover the pan, then cook for 3-4 minutes and stir again. Continue cooking and stirring until the potatoes are cooked and lightly browned. Serve immediately.

# GOBI MATTAR (CABBAGE WITH GARDEN PEAS)

*I always think of peas as the perfect accompaniment to lamb and therefore recommend serving this with any lamb curry. The dish is more colourful if you use a green cabbage such as savoy, rather than white.*

Serves 4-6

*INGREDIENTS*
340g/12oz green cabbage
3 tbsps cooking oil
¼ tsp black mustard seeds
½ tsp cumin seeds
10-12 fenugreek seeds (optional)
2-4 dried red chillies, whole
1 small onion, finely sliced
½ tsp ground turmeric
120g/4oz frozen peas
¾ tsp salt
1 tsp ground coriander
¼-½ tsp chilli powder
2 small ripe tomatoes, skinned and chopped
1 tbsp freshly chopped coriander leaves (optional)

Shred or chop the cabbage finely. Heat the oil over a medium heat and fry the mustard seeds until they pop. Add the cumin seeds, fenugreek (if using), red chillies and the onions. Stir and fry until the onions are soft. Stir in the turmeric and add the cabbage. Mix thoroughly then add the peas and salt. Cover the pan, reduce the heat to minimum and cook for 5 minutes. Add the ground coriander, chilli powder and the chopped tomatoes and stir-fry until completely dry.

Remove the pan from the heat and stir in half the coriander leaves. Turn the cabbage into a warmed serving dish and garnish with the remaining coriander leaves.

# ALOO KI BHAJI
# (SPICED POTATOES)

*I always enjoy the combination of potatoes and onions,*
*enhanced in this dish by whole spices and chillies.*

Serves 4-6

### INGREDIENTS
680g/1½lbs potatoes
5-6 tbsps cooking oil
½ tsp black mustard seeds
2-3 dried red chillies
⅛ tsp fenugreek seeds
225g/8oz onions, finely sliced
1-2 fresh green chillies, sliced
  lengthways and seeded if a
  milder flavour is preferred
1 tsp ground turmeric
1 tsp salt
30g/1oz freshly chopped
  coriander leaves

Boil the potatoes in their skins
then allow them to cool
thoroughly. Peel the potatoes
and dice them evenly.

Heat the oil over a medium heat
in a wide shallow pan and fry
the mustard seeds until they pop.
Add the red chillies and the
fenugreek seeds; then the onions
and green chillies. Fry until the
onions are golden brown. Add
the turmeric, potatoes and salt.
Stir and fry gently until the
potatoes are heated through,
then stir in the coriander leaves
and serve.

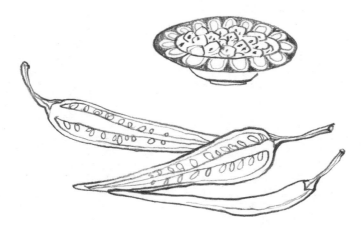

# ALOO-MATTAR AND MIRCHI BHAJI (POTATO, PEA AND GREEN PEPPER CURRY)

*This potato and pea curry is unusual as it also includes green pepper – this makes it refreshingly different!*

Serves 4

### INGREDIENTS
1 onion, chopped
60g/2oz ghee *or* 2 tbsps oil
2 potatoes, peeled and diced
1 tsp ground coriander
1 tsp chilli powder
¼ tsp ground turmeric
225g/8oz frozen peas
1 green pepper, seeded and cut
    into pieces
200g/7oz can chopped tomatoes
Salt
2 green chillies, cut into quarters
1 tbsp freshly chopped coriander
120ml/4 fl oz water

Fry the onion in the ghee or oil until softened then add the potatoes and fry for 5-6 minutes. Add the ground coriander, chilli powder and turmeric, mix well and add the peas and green pepper. Stir, add the tomato and season with salt. Add the chopped green chillies, fresh coriander and water, cover and cook for 5-6 minutes until the potatoes are tender.

# GOBI ALOO (CAULIFLOWER & POTATOES)

*This is a truly classic Indian side dish, and one of the best known. A slow cooking with spices gives a subtle but distinctive flavour.*

Serves 4-6

### INGREDIENTS
3 potatoes
1 cauliflower
5 tbsps cooking oil
½ tsp black mustard seeds
½ tsp cumin seeds
12-15 fenugreek seeds
1-2 dried red chillies, roughly chopped
1 onion, roughly chopped
1 fresh green chilli, roughly chopped
½ tsp ground turmeric
½ tsp ground cumin
1 tsp ground coriander
1¼ tsps salt
1 tbsp freshly chopped coriander leaves (optional)

Boil the potatoes in their skins and allow to cool thoroughly. Peel the potatoes and cut them into 5cm/2 inch dice. Blanch the cauliflower in boiling water for 2 minutes. Do not over-boil as it should remain firm after cooking. Allow the cauliflower to cool and then cut it into 1.25cm/½ inch florets.

Heat the oil over a medium heat in a wide shallow pan, preferably non-stick or cast iron. Add the mustard seeds, and as soon as they begin to pop, add the cumin and fenugreek seeds and the red chillies. Add the onions and the green chilli, stir and fry until the onions are golden brown. Add the cauliflower, reduce the heat to low, cover the pan and cook for 6-8 minutes. Add the potatoes, turmeric, cumin, coriander and salt. Stir gently until all the ingredients are thoroughly mixed. Cover the pan and cook for 5-6 minutes until the potatoes are heated through. Stir in the coriander leaves and serve immediately.

# GREEN BEAN BHAJI

*For best results use frozen beans for this bhaji – the ice will help to make just the right amount of liquor for serving with the beans.*

Serves 4

### INGREDIENTS
3 tbsps oil
1 tsp urid dhal
2-3 green chillies
6-8 fresh curry leaves
340g/12oz frozen sliced green beans
Salt to taste
1 tbsp desiccated coconut

Heat the oil and add the urid dhal, green chilli and curry leaves. Stir-fry for half a minute then add the beans and sprinkle with salt. Cover and cook for 6-8 minutes. Add the coconut and mix well. Cover and cook for 3-4 minutes. Serve with chapatis.

# TOORAI TARKARI
# (COURGETTE CURRY)

*This is a tasty side dish at any time of the year but is especially good to make when courgettes and tomatoes are plentiful in the garden.*

Serves 4

*INGREDIENTS*
1½ tbsps oil
1 tsp cumin seeds
225g/8oz courgettes, peeled and
  sliced into 6mm/¼ inch rounds
½ tsp chilli powder
1 tsp ground coriander
¼ tsp turmeric powder
3-4 fresh or canned tomatoes,
  chopped
Salt to taste
1 green chilli, halved
1 tbsp freshly chopped coriander
  leaves

Heat the oil and add the cumin seeds. When they start to pop, add the courgette slices. Stir and add the ground chilli, coriander and turmeric powder. Mix well and add the chopped tomatoes, salt, green chilli and fresh coriander. Cover and cook for 10-12 minutes. Add extra salt if necessary and serve immediately.

# KHATA-MEETHA KADDU (SWEET AND SOUR PUMPKIN)

*Pumpkin is a very versatile vegetable – once you try it you are easily hooked! It stays moist during cooking, allowing this to be a moist curry yet without any sauce.*

Serves 4

## INGREDIENTS
60g/2oz ghee *or* 3 tbsps oil
1 bay leaf
2.5cm/1 inch cinnamon stick
6 green cardamoms
6 cloves
1 tsp five-spice mixture (panchphoran)
2 potatoes, peeled and diced
460g/1lb pumpkin, peeled and diced
1 tsp chilli powder
1½ tsps ground coriander
¼ tsp ground turmeric
½ tsp salt
2 tsps sugar
1 tbsp tamarind pulp
3 tbsps water

Heat the ghee or oil and add the bay leaf, cinnamon, cardamoms, cloves and five-spice mixture – fry for 30 seconds. Add the potatoes and fry for 4 minutes, then add the pumpkin. Stir the vegetables and cook for 3 minutes, then add the chilli powder, coriander, turmeric, salt and sugar. Stir, then add the tamarind pulp and water. Cover and cook over a gentle heat for 8-10 minutes, until the potatoes are tender.

# PALAK PANEER
# (PANEER AND SPINACH)

*Paneer is an Indian cheese. Use a cheese such as halloumi in its place if it is not available.*

Serves 4

*INGREDIENTS*
460g/1lb fresh spinach leaf *or* 225g/8oz frozen chopped spinach defrosted
60g/2oz ghee *or* 3 tbsps oil
225g/8oz paneer, diced
1 onion, finely chopped
2.5cm/1 inch piece fresh root ginger, peeled and finely chopped
4 fresh tomatoes *or* 4-5 canned tomatoes, chopped
1 tsp chilli powder
1 tsp ground coriander
¼ tsp ground turmeric
¼ tsp salt
1 tbsp lemon juice
30g/1oz unsalted butter

Boil the fresh spinach in 570ml/1 pint of water for 5 minutes. Drain and reserve the water. Chop or purée the spinach and set to one side. If canned or thawed frozen spinach is used, save the liquid.

Heat the ghee or oil in a large pan and fry the paneer pieces until lightly browned. Remove with a slotted spoon and set to one side. In the same oil, fry the onion and ginger for 3-4 minutes, add the tomatoes, then chilli, coriander, turmeric and salt to taste. Cover and cook for 2-3 minutes. Add the paneer, puréed spinach and lemon juice. If the mixture is too dry add 2-3 tbsps spinach water to moisten the curry. Remove from heat and serve with butter.

# ALOO METHI
# (POTATO AND FRESH
# FENUGREEK LEAVES)

*This vegetable side dish is best made with fenugreek leaves
but coriander could be used as a substitute.*

Serves 3-4

*INGREDIENTS*
60g/2oz ghee *or* 3 tbsps oil
1 tsp cumin seeds
1 pinch asafoetida (hing)
3 potatoes, peeled and cut into
  chunks
1 bunch fresh fenugreek (methi)
  leaves, chopped
1 tsp chilli powder
1 tsp coriander powder
Salt
¼ tsp turmeric powder
Juice of 1 lemon

Heat the ghee or oil in a large
frying pan and add the cumin
seeds and asafoetida. When the
seeds start to pop, add the
potatoes. Fry for 3-4 minutes
then add the fenugreek (methi)
leaves. Mix well and add the
chilli powder, coriander, salt and
turmeric, stirring well. Cover and
cook over a low heat for 6-8
minutes. Add the lemon juice
before serving.

# SALADS, SAUCES & CHUTNEYS

The classic Indian way of serving salad vegetables is raw in side dishes, providing a contrast to meat and vegetables dishes cooked and served in rich sauces. How dull a starter of popadoms and chutney would be without a simple salad of tomato and onion to serve with it.

Indian markets are the most colourful of places, to both the eye and to the nose! Spices, essential to all Indian dishes, are sold from sacks amidst piles of fresh herbs and a staggering array of colourful fruits and vegetables. Many of the vegetables make refreshing salads, but some may require a little explanation for the novice curry cook.

## Mooli – Peppery but Mild

A salad vegetable widely available in most western supermarkets but perhaps requiring a little explanation is the mooli – a long white radish, also known as daikon in Oriental cookery. It is pungent when cut, especially when grated as this allows much of the juice to flow freely, but the actual flavour is surprisingly mild. The white flesh of the mooli provides a stunning colour contrast to brightly coloured vegetables such as carrots and the mild, slightly peppery flavour blends well with just about every salad vegetable – I love it with watercress, but that is not a classic Indian combination! A word of warning – store grated mooli in an air-tight box in the refrigerator; plastic wrap is rather too permeable to confine the aroma.

## An Essential in any Meal

Pickles and chutneys add so much extra flavour to Indian meals; they might be spicy relishes or cooling sauces depending on the ingredients used. They were traditionally home-made, but the marvellous range of authentic pickles and chutneys that are now commercially available, combined with a different life-style for the Indian women of today, means that relatively few people still make chutneys at home. However raitas, mild yogurt sauces flavoured with salad vegetables and served as an accompaniment to many spicy dishes and fried starters, are best when home-made on the day that they are to be eaten.

## No-cook Dressings for the Perfect Finishing Touch

Raitas are like the vast majority of salads – they generally involve no cooking and are just a mixing together of various ingredients. A few spices may occasionally require roasting to enhance their flavour before being added to the yogurt, but that is about it in terms of cooking. Cucumber, carrot and onion raitas are all made in this way but there are some interesting variations which do actually require the vegetables to be cooked – recipes for potato, okra and aubergine raitas are included in this chapter and are well worth the preparation required for a special Indian meal – the texture of fried vegetables within a raita is delicious.

## Quick-cook Chutneys

There is quite a difference between a chutney and a pickle in Indian cookery – chutneys are usually mild and pickles, frequently cooked in oil, vary between hot and exceptionally hot and should be treated with the utmost respect!

The chutneys included here are mild and fragrant, often little more than sauces but adding a lightness and freshness to an Indian meal. Two of them really set my taste buds tingling! The Avocado Chutney recipe is very similar to a Mexican guacamole but without the garlic and tomato. A little heat is provided by the chopped green chilli but the overall taste sensation is mild and creamy, and the chutney is delicious with chicken dishes and dhals. Green Coriander Chutney combines all the brightness and fragrance of leaf coriander with the delicate flavour of coconut and the traditional Indian seasonings of garlic, chillies and ginger. Try to buy the coriander in a greengrocers or an Indian grocers – an ounce of leaves in plastic packets from the supermarket will be very expensive although, I have to say, in my opinion the taste justifies the cost!

Most of the chutneys included in this chapter are for immediate consumption but any left-overs may be kept in the refrigerator for a few days, or as specified in the recipe. The Red Hot Chutney, and others requiring a long cook and storage to allow them to mature, should be bottled in clean glass jars, dried in a warm oven and filled when both the jars and the chutney are hot. Always cover chutneys with lids and not cellophane tops – this prevents any evaporation from the chutney, which may lead to it drying out during storage.

# KACHHOOMAR (SHREDDED ONION SALAD)

*Cut the onion into rings for the most attractive presentation of this salad. I serve this with popadoms and chutneys as an easy starter.*

Serves 4

### INGREDIENTS
1 large Spanish onion, finely sliced
¼ tsp salt
¼ tsp chilli powder
1 tbsp freshly chopped coriander leaves
1 green chilli, chopped
1 tbsp lemon juice
2 fresh tomatoes, chopped (optional)

Place all the ingredients in a bowl and toss together to mix. Leave for 10 minutes, so that the juice from the onions starts to run, then serve with kababs, curries or pakoras.

# CARROT AND COCONUT SALAD

*Coconut is often used in curries – the association of carrots with Indian food is less obvious. This salad is light and refreshing – the perfect accompaniment to the hotter curries such as vindaloos.*

Serves 4-6

*INGREDIENTS*
225g/8oz carrots
2 tbsps desiccated coconut
30g/1oz finely shredded onion
1 tbsp lemon juice
2 tbsps freshly chopped
  coriander leaves
1 fresh green chilli, seeded and
  roughly chopped (optional)
½ tsp salt

Peel and grate the carrots, then combine all the ingredients except the salt in a bowl. Stir in the salt just before serving.

197

# KASSI MOOLI
# (GRATED MOOLI)

*A simple salad, but one with a strong aroma! Mooli actually taste quite mild but have a very distinctive fragrance – wrap the salad well or store in an air-tight box and keep it in the refrigerator.*

Serves 4

### INGREDIENTS
225g/8oz mooli
Salt
Juice of 1 lemon
1 green chilli, finely chopped
1 tbsp freshly chopped coriander

Wash and peel the mooli, then grate it. Place the grated mooli in a sieve, press lightly and allow some of the liquid to drain away, then transfer the mooli to a serving dish.

Sprinkle the mooli with salt and lemon juice and mix in the chilli and coriander.

# NARANGI PIYAZ SALAD (ONION AND ORANGE SALAD)

*This side salad is delicious – a refreshing and unusual blend of flavours. Use corn oil or vegetable oil for the dressing.*

Serves 4

*INGREDIENTS*

2 large seedless oranges *or* 4
  satsumas
6 spring onions, finely chopped,
  including the green leaves
Salt
2 tsps lemon juice
¼ tsp freshly ground black
  pepper
½ tsp sugar
2 tsps salad oil

Peel the oranges and cut or break them into segments – cut the segments into 2 if they are large. Add the spring onions, salt, lemon juice, pepper, sugar and oil and toss the salad gently, combining the oranges and onions with the dressing.

# CABBAGE AND MINT SALAD

*The mint sauce used to dress this salad gives it a vivid colour and strong flavour.*

Serves 4-6

*INGREDIENTS*
280-340g/10-12oz white cabbage
1 small onion, finely chopped
1 fresh green chilli, finely
   chopped, seeded if a milder
   flavour is preferred
2-3 tbsps thick-set natural yogurt
2 tsps mint sauce
½ tsp salt

Grate the cabbage or shred it very finely, then place it in a large mixing bowl. Add the rest of the ingredients and mix thoroughly. Place the salad in a serving dish, cover and chill before serving.

# TOMATO AND CUCUMBER SALAD

*This makes a colourful side dish to serve with almost any curry. The peanuts add colour and texture to the salad.*

Serves 4-6

### INGREDIENTS
½ cucumber
2 tomatoes
1 bunch spring onions, roughly
  chopped
1 tbsp lemon juice
1 tbsp olive oil
¼ tsp salt
¼ tsp freshly ground black
  pepper
1 tbsp freshly chopped coriander
  leaves
30g/1oz roasted salted peanuts,
  crushed

Peel the cucumber and chop it finely. Chop the tomatoes finely, then place the cucumber, tomatoes and spring onions into a serving bowl.

Combine the lemon juice, olive oil, salt, pepper and coriander leaves and set to one side. Combine all the ingredients just before serving.

# SMOKED MACKEREL SALAD

*Smoked mackerel works well in this salad which would be made with home-smoked fish in India. The marinated fish may be served on small savoury biscuits as a cocktail snack.*

Serves 4

### INGREDIENTS
225g/8oz smoked mackerel
60g/2oz finely chopped onions
1 fresh green chilli, seeded and
   finely chopped
2 tbsps freshly chopped
   coriander leaves
1½ tbsps lemon juice

Remove the skin and bones from the fish and flake the flesh with a fork. Add all the remaining ingredients and mix thoroughly. Cover and refrigerate for 2-3 hours before serving on a salad garnish.

# CARROT AND MOOLI SALAD

*Mooli, a white radish, is now widely available in supermarkets and specialist greengrocers. This makes an excellent side dish to serve with any but the creamiest curries.*

Serves 4-6

### INGREDIENTS
1 tbsp cooking oil
½ tsp black mustard seeds
½ tsp cumin seeds
120g/4oz carrots, peeled and
  coarsely grated
225g/8oz mooli, peeled and
  coarsely grated
½ tsp salt
2-3 tbsps finely chopped onion
1 tbsp lemon juice
1 tbsp finely chopped coriander
  leaves

Heat the oil over medium heat and fry the mustard seeds until they pop, add the cumin and remove from heat. Add the grated carrots and mooli and allow to cool. Stir in the salt, onion, lemon juice and coriander leaves before serving.

# POTATO RAITA

*In this unusual raita lightly cooked potato is cooled before being added to spiced yogurt.*

Serves 4-6

### INGREDIENTS
2 tbsps cooking oil
¼ tsp fennel seeds
1 clove garlic, peeled and finely chopped
225g/8oz potatoes, peeled and diced
½ tsp ground cumin
½ tsp salt
150g/5oz natural yogurt
½ tsp sugar
¼ tsp chilli powder or paprika

Heat the oil over a medium heat and fry the fennel seeds until they are brown. Add the garlic and allow it to turn slightly brown, then add the potatoes and stir. Cover the pan and cook until the potatoes are tender and brown, stirring frequently. Stir in the cumin and salt, mix thoroughly and remove from the heat. Allow to cool completely.

Beat the yogurt and sugar until smooth. Add the spiced potatoes with any oil that remains in the pan. Stir and mix well. Place the raita in a serving dish and sprinkle with the chilli powder or paprika before serving.

# CUCUMBER RAITA

*This is a very mild, refreshing raita, lightly spiced with
roasted cumin seeds.*

Serves 4-6

### INGREDIENTS
1 small cucumber
1 tsp cumin seeds
150g/5oz thick-set natural yogurt
¼ tsp salt
¼ tsp paprika

Peel the cucumber and cut lengthways into two halves. Slice each half finely. Heat a small pan over a low heat and dry roast the cumin seeds until they turn a shade darker. Allow the seeds to cool, then crush them with a rolling pin or in a pestle and mortar.

Beat the yogurt until smooth, then stir in the cumin with the salt. Reserve a few slices of cucumber for garnish and add the rest to the yogurt – mix thoroughly. Place the raita in a serving dish and arrange the reserved cucumber on top. Sprinkle the paprika evenly over the sliced cucumber.

# BHINDI (OKRA) RAITA

*Fried bhindi are crisp and not sticky – the texture of stewed okra can be off-putting. This is an unusual, spicy raita.*

Serves 6-8

### INGREDIENTS
Oil for deep-frying
225g/8oz bhindi (okra), cut into
  very thin slices
½ tsp salt
1 fresh green chilli, seeded and
  roughly chopped
150g/5oz thick-set natural yogurt
½ tsp mustard powder
1 tbsp cooking oil
½ tsp black mustard seeds
1 tbsp curry leaves

Deep-fry the bhindi until they are well browned and crisp. Drain on absorbent kitchen paper then allow to cool completely.

Add the salt to the green chilli and crush to a pulp. Beat the yogurt with a fork until smooth, then add the mustard powder and the green chilli mixture, stir and mix well. Gently stir in the fried bhindi.

Heat the 1 tbsp oil in a small pan and fry the mustard seeds until they crackle, then add the curry leaves and fry for 15-20 seconds. Remove the pan from the heat and stir the seasoned oil into the bhindi raita with all the seasonings. Serve lightly chilled.

# MINT AND ONION RAITA

*Made with bottled mint this raita has a most astonishing,
bright green colour. I prefer to use fresh garden mint when
possible.*

Serves 4-6

### INGREDIENTS
150g/5oz thick-set natural yogurt
1 small onion, finely chopped
1 tbsp freshly chopped fresh
  mint, *or* 1 tsp bottled garden
  mint with ½ tsp sugar
1 fresh green chilli, seeded and
  chopped
½ tsp salt
¼ tsp paprika

Beat the yogurt until smooth.
Add the remaining ingredients,
except the paprika, and beat
again. Place the raita in a serving
dish and sprinkle with the
paprika before serving.

# CARROT AND PEANUT RAITA

*A colourful and highly nutritious raita, ideal for serving with vegetable curries.*

Serves 4-6

### INGREDIENTS

2 carrots
60g/2oz roasted salted peanuts
1 small clove of garlic, peeled and roughly chopped
1 fresh green chilli, seeded and roughly chopped
¼ tsp salt
150g/5oz thick-set natural yogurt
½ tsp sugar
1 tbsp freshly chopped coriander leaves

Peel and grate the carrots coarsely. Crush the peanuts with a pestle and mortar or a rolling pin. Mix the garlic, chilli and salt and crush to a pulp.

Beat the yogurt until smooth and stir in the garlic mixture. Add the carrots, peanuts, sugar and coriander leaves and mix thoroughly. Chill and serve.

# CUCUMBER AND ONION RAITA

*This is one of the most popular, and cooling, raitas or yogurt sauces. Add more or less onion, to taste.*

Serves 4-6

INGREDIENTS
1 tsp cumin seeds
150g/5oz natural yogurt
3 tbsps finely chopped onions
½ cucumber, peeled and finely
   chopped
½ tsp salt

Heat a cast iron or heavy-based pan and dry-roast the cumin seeds until they release their aroma. Allow to cool then crush them lightly in a pestle and mortar.

Beat the yogurt with a fork until smooth, then add the remaining ingredients and half the crushed cumin seeds. Mix thoroughly. Place the raita in a serving dish and scatter the remaining cumin seeds on top.

# AUBERGINE RAITA

*All raitas are quite cooling – they are good to have to hand if your curry is hotter than planned! Cook the aubergine for the full 10 minutes or the flesh will be difficult to mash.*

Serves 6-8

### INGREDIENTS

1 aubergine weighing about 340g/12oz

½ tsp salt

1.25cm/½ inch piece of fresh root ginger, peeled and roughly chopped

1 fresh green chilli, roughly chopped and seeded for a milder flavour

150g/5oz thick-set natural yogurt

2-3 tbsps finely chopped onions

2 tbsps freshly chopped coriander leaves

Make one or two small incisions in the aubergine to prevent it from bursting during cooking.

Preheat the grill to medium. Grill the whole aubergine for 10 minutes, turning it over once. Allow it to cool completely.

Add the salt to the ginger and green chilli and crush them to a pulp. Cut the aubergine lengthways into two halves and scoop out the flesh. Chop the flesh finely or mash it. Beat the yogurt until smooth. Add the ginger and chilli pulp and mix well. Add the aubergine and mix thoroughly. Stir in the onions and half the coriander leaves just before serving. Garnish with the remaining coriander.

# DATE SAUCE

*This is a sweet and sour relish to serve with kababs, pakoras or any snack. Tamarind is easiest to use in concentrate form.*

Serves 6-8

*INGREDIENTS*
60g/2oz pitted dates
15g/½oz seedless raisins
1 tsp ground cumin
1 tsp chilli powder
1 tsp tamarind concentrate *or* 3
   tbsps lemon juice
¾ tsp salt
1 tsp soft brown sugar
120ml/4 fl oz cold water

Place all the ingredients in a liquidiser with half the water. Process until the ingredients are half blended then add the remaining water and blend until fairly smooth. Pour the sauce into a sieve and press it through with a metal spoon until only a dry and coarse mixture is left in the sieve – discard this mixture and transfer the sauce to a serving bowl.

# ONION RELISH

*I often find raw onions too strong so I suggest washing the onions for this relish before adding them to the other ingredients.*

Serves 4-6

## INGREDIENTS
225g/8oz onions, finely chopped
1 fresh green chilli, seeded and
   minced
1 tbsp fresh mint, minced
1 tbsp fresh coriander leaves,
   minced
1 tbsp lemon juice
½ tsp salt

Mix all the ingredients together except the salt. Add the salt just before serving. This will prevent the relish from becoming too wet before it is served.

# GREEN CORIANDER
# CHUTNEY

*How did we enliven our food before leaf coriander was*
*widely available? This glorious chutney celebrates the fresh*
*flavour of coriander leaves.*

Serves 6-8

### INGREDIENTS
175ml/6 fl oz water
30g/1oz desiccated coconut
1-2 fresh green chillies, chopped,
  seeded if a milder flavour is
  preferred
1-2 cloves garlic, peeled and
  roughly chopped
1.25cm/½-inch piece of fresh
  root ginger, peeled and
  roughly chopped
30g/1oz freshly chopped
  coriander leaves
½ tsp salt
1 tbsp lemon juice

Bring the water to the boil,
remove it from the heat and soak
the coconut in the water for 10-
15 minutes. Place all the
ingredients in a liquidiser or food
processor and blend until
smooth. Allow to cool
completely.

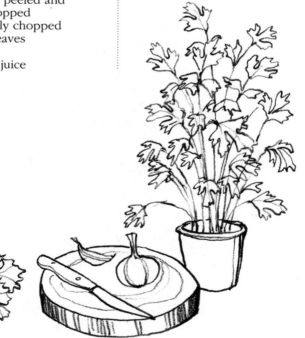

# AVOCADO CHUTNEY

*I love the creamy rich flavour of avocado. It blends easily with garlic, chilli and coriander to make a delicious sauce or chutney.*

Serves 6-8

*INGREDIENTS*
1 ripe avocado
Juice of ½ lemon
60g/2oz plain cottage cheese
1 clove garlic, peeled and
  chopped
2 tbsps freshly chopped
  coriander leaves
1 fresh green chilli, chopped,
  seeded if a milder flavour is
  preferred
½ tsp salt

Cut the avocado into two and remove the stone. Scoop out the flesh. Place the lemon juice in a liquidiser or food processor and add the avocado with all the remaining ingredients. Blend until smooth, adding a little water if necessary. Taste, add a little extra salt if necessary, and chill until required.

# APPLE CHUTNEY

*This fruity chutney is quite highly spiced and makes a
perfect accompaniment to all Indian snacks and starters.
Store the chutney in the refrigerator.*

Serves 8-10

### INGREDIENTS

1 tbsp cooking oil
½ tsp black mustard seeds
¼ tsp fenugreek seeds
¼ tsp ground turmeric
Pinch of asaphoetida (optional)
2 large cooking apples, peeled
  and finely chopped
½-¾ tsp chilli powder
1½ tsps salt
3 tbsps soft light brown sugar

Heat the oil over a medium heat
and fry the mustard seeds until
they pop. Add the fenugreek,
turmeric and asaphoetida, then
the apples. Stir and mix
thoroughly. Add the chilli
powder, salt and sugar, stir and
cook until the apple starts to
soften. Cover and simmer until
the apple is tender, stirring
frequently. Allow the chutney to
cool. Store in a screw-top jar in
the refrigerator for 4-6 weeks.

# CUMIN-CORIANDER CHUTNEY

*This is a mild chutney to serve with pakoras or any starter or snack. The raw onions are actually dominated by the spices, especially the cumin.*

Serves 4-6

### INGREDIENTS
1 tsp cumin seeds
1 tsp coriander seeds
2-3 dried red chillies
4 tbsps desiccated coconut
60ml/2 fl oz water
½ tsp salt
1½ tbsps lemon juice
2-3 tbsps finely chopped onions

Grind the cumin, coriander, red chillies and coconut in a pestle and mortar or a coffee grinder until the ingredients are smooth. Transfer to a bowl and add the water, salt and lemon juice. Mix thoroughly, then stir in the finely chopped onions.

# MINT AND ONION CHUTNEY

*This is a light chutney, more like a marmalade. It will keep for several weeks in an air-tight container or jar in the refrigerator.*

Serves 6-8

## INGREDIENTS
2 tbsps cooking oil
1 large onion, roughly chopped
15g/½oz fresh mint
1 fresh green chilli, seeded if a
  milder flavour is preferred
1 tbsp lemon juice
½ tsp salt

Heat the oil over a medium heat and fry the onion until soft but not brown. Allow to cool. Place the onion and the rest of the ingredients in a liquidiser or food processor and blend until smooth. Store in an airtight container or screw-top jar in the refrigerator.

# MEETHI TOMATAR CHUTNEY (SWEET TOMATO CHUTNEY)

*This tomato chutney is only lightly spiced and quite delicious. Bottle it immediately or store any surplus in the refrigerator.*

### INGREDIENTS
30g/1oz ghee *or* 1 tbsp oil
2.5cm/1 inch cinnamon stick
1 bay leaf
6 cloves
1 tsp mustard seeds
1 tsp chilli powder
¼ tsp turmeric powder
60g/2oz sugar
460g/1lb fresh or canned
   tomatoes
60g/2oz raisins
½ tsp salt

Heat the ghee or oil and fry the cinnamon, bay leaf and cloves for 1 minute. Add the mustard seeds and when they start to pop, add the chilli, turmeric and sugar. Mix well and add the tomatoes. Mix well and add the raisins and salt. Cover and simmer for 8-10 minutes. Add a little water if necessary.

# ADRAK KHAJOOR KI KHATI MITHI CHUTNEY (DATE AND GINGER CHUTNEY)

*This sweet, spicy chutney is ideal with meat or chicken curries. It may be bottled and kept for up to 3 months, in or out of the refrigerator.*

### INGREDIENTS

120g/4oz dates, sliced and pitted
60g/2oz fresh root ginger, peeled
  and cut into matchsticks
120g/4oz fresh, unripe mango,
  peeled and thinly sliced *or*
  60g/2oz dry mango pieces
  (aamchur)
60g/2oz raisins and currants,
  mixed
30g/1oz almonds, chopped
200ml/7 fl oz water
175g/6oz sugar or grated jaggery
¼ tsp salt
1 tsp chilli powder

Place the dates, ginger, fresh or dry mango, currants and almonds in a saucepan, and add the water. Leave for 6-8 minutes. Add the sugar or grated jaggery, salt and chilli powder and bring gently to the boil. Simmer for 15-20 minutes until the chutney is thick and sticky. Remove, cool and serve.

# TMALI KI CHUTNEY
# (TAMARIND CHUTNEY)

*Tamarind Chutney goes really well with kababs. It keeps in the refrigerator for up to a month. Tamarind is a sticky paste or pulp – the tamarind is sometimes called the Indian date. You will find it in specialist Indian shops.*

Serves 6-8

## INGREDIENTS

225g/8oz dry tamarind pods
120-175g/4-6oz sugar or grated
    jaggery
¼ tsp salt
1 tsp chilli powder
1 tsp cumin seeds
1 tsp coriander seeds

Soak the tamarind pods in 150ml/¼ pint of boiling water for 5 minutes. Squeeze the pods to remove the soft pulp. Strain through a sieve or squeeze dry by hand. Add a little fresh warm water to the pulp and repeat the process 3 times. The first extract is the thickest and subsequent ones will be thinner and milder. Take 225-250ml/8-9 fl oz of thick tamarind extract, and discard the pods. Add the sugar or jaggery, salt and chilli powder. Lightly roast the cumin and coriander seeds in a dry frying pan and cook over a low heat until lightly browned. Grind the spices, add to the tamarind mixture and mix well. Adjust the sugar and salt if necessary.

# NAU-RATTAN CHUTNEY (NINE JEWELLED CHUTNEY)

*This is a chutney to bottle and keep, and to use as required. It is quite thick and sticky.*

### INGREDIENTS
1 banana, sliced
1 apple, cored and chopped
1 large mango, peeled, stoned and sliced
3 rings of canned pineapple, chopped
200-225g/7-8oz canned peaches, drained and chopped
120g/4oz dates, pitted and sliced
60g/2oz fresh root ginger, peeled and chopped
60g/2oz raisins
175-200g/6-7oz brown sugar or jaggery
2-3 dry red chillies
175ml/6 fl oz malt vinegar
1 tsp salt
½ tsp cumin seeds
½ tsp coriander seeds
½ tsp onion seeds
½ tsp aniseed seeds
60g/2oz almonds, chopped

Place all the fruits, dates, ginger, raisins, sugar, chillies and malt vinegar in a large saucepan. Add the salt and simmer gently for 10-15 minutes.

Place all the whole spices in a dry frying pan and cook over a low heat until lightly browned. Allow to cool and then grind in a pestle and mortar. Add coarsely ground spices and the almonds. Mix well and cook for 5-6 minutes. Cool slightly and bottle.

# LAL MIREH AUR MOONG PHALI CHUTNEY (RED-HOT CHUTNEY)

*This chutney can be as 'red-hot' as you like – add more or less red chillies to taste! The red pepper gives lots of colour to the dish and the peanuts add texture.*

Serves 4

### INGREDIENTS
1 large red pepper
3-4 whole dried red chillies
60g/2oz unsalted peanuts
1.25cm/½ inch piece fresh root
   ginger, peeled and sliced
Juice of 3 lemons
Salt

Cut the red pepper in half, remove the pith and seeds. Place it in a liquidiser or food processor with the chillies, peanuts and ginger and blend until smooth. A few spoons of lemon juice may be needed to blend the mixture. Pour into a bowl. Add the salt and the lemon juice, mix well and serve.

# DAHI-PODINA CHUTNEY (YOGURT AND MINT CHUTNEY)

*This is a very simple chutney or raita to serve with any number of curries. Ready-made mint sauce may be used in place of fresh or dried mint.*

Serves 4

*INGREDIENTS*
150ml/¼ pint natural yogurt
4 tsps sugar
1 tbsp freshly chopped mint *or* 2
   tsps dried mint powder
Salt

Place the yogurt, sugar and mint in a liquidiser or food processor and blend for 1-2 minutes. Add the salt and mix.

# DESSERTS & DRINKS

Desserts are not all that common in India – sweetmeats and sweet dishes are eaten but more as snacks during the day than as the final course of a meal. However, for banquets and feast days Indians delight in sweet dishes, which are often lavishly decorated in wealthy households with edible gold or silver leaf.

## Any Excuse is a Good Excuse

A new baby, exam results, a visitor, someone going away – any excuse is a good excuse for a celebration and sweetmeats are the real celebratory foods of India. They are occasionally made at home but the markets are full of stalls selling fudges, halvas

224

and other milk-based delicacies. Modern stores sell such foods clinically packaged but most people would prefer to seek out the traditional experts in this field, the *halvais*, who sell their goods from stalls or open-fronted shops in the markets. Many sweetmeats are time-consuming and complicated to prepare, so Indian logic says leave it to the experts!

## Rich and Creamy Milk Puddings

Most of the milk used in Indian cookery is full fat – when I have made Indian desserts at home I find that the best results are achieved using gold top or Channel Islands milk. The milk is often boiled for a considerable time to evaporate some of the whey, leaving an even thicker, richer liquid. For convenience, the recipes for halva and firni in this chapter use canned evaporated milk. Other recipes actually specify full-cream milk and you should be certain to use this to achieve the correct consistency and the best possible result.

Indian milk puddings often contain nuts, and pistachios are particularly popular, for both their flavour and colour. Cardamom seeds are the most common spice used in sweet dishes but the more typical flavourings for desserts are light and fragrant – flower waters are widely used.

Vermicelli and rice are both used extensively in desserts but the resulting puddings are usually served cold – in most other cuisines rice or macaroni puddings would be served hot. These puddings are more highly spiced than many others and, indeed, they rely on the spices for any flavour that they have. Puddings which are mainly milk and semolina or ground almonds are popular in India but seldom appeal to western tastes.

## Fabulous Exotic Fruits

Mangoes, pineapples, bananas and coconuts – fruits that sound exotic to us are common place in India and are frequently eaten either by themselves or made into sorbets or sherbets. There is absolutely no comparison between a fruit such as a mango which is grown, ripened and eaten in the same country and a fruit that is picked and then transported half way round the world, slowly ripening under refrigeration. One of my favourite desserts in this chapter is Melon Balls in Mango Purée – the combination of flavours is exceptional but both fruits need to be fully ripe to produce the best results.

### Halva, a Popular Indian Sweetmeat

I have always thought of halva as a sweetmeat made from sesame seeds and originating in the Middle East. However, the Indians make what they call halva from a milk-based mixture, often flavoured with vegetables such as carrots as well as nuts and sugar. The recipe for Carrot Halva is particularly popular and is traditionally served as part of a celebratory meal, decorated with edible gold leaf, whereas the Semolina and Almond Halva is more suitable for everyday eating.

### Refreshing Drinks of Fruit or Spice

The most famous of all Indian drinks must surely be tea (see recipe for Spiced Tea) but many other drinks are made from fruits or spices. There is also an up-and-coming brewing industry and Indian beers are now widely available in western supermarkets – most people drinking alcohol prefer to drink beer with Indian food rather than wine. The very popular southern Indian drink of Rasam is made from a lightly spiced infusion of red lentils and is served warm – a far cry from a traditional western lemonade or fruit juice! Rasam is usually served as a drink although some may prefer to present it as a thin soup which may be sipped throughout a meal.

Most fruit drinks require chilling for at least two hours before serving – I find this is especially important when serving drinks based on mangoes. A mango as a fruit at room temperature is refreshingly juicy and delicious. Served as a drink at the same temperature it is dull and insipidly sweet.

# CARROT HALVA

*Halva is very sweet and very popular. This recipe for carrot halva is most unusual.*

Serves 6

### INGREDIENTS

900g/2lbs carrots, peeled and grated
430ml/¾ pint evaporated milk
150g/5oz sugar
2.5cm/1 inch piece cinnamon stick
2 bay leaves
60g/2oz blanched almonds, chopped
120g/4oz unsalted butter
8 green cardamoms, seeds removed and crushed
30g/1oz pistachio nuts, chopped

Place the carrots, milk and sugar in a heavy-based saucepan, with the cinnamon stick and bay leaves. Cook over a low heat, until the liquid has almost completely evaporated. Stir in the almonds, butter and cardamom seeds. Continue cooking over the low heat, stirring continuously, until the mixture in the pan changes colour from orange to a deep red or brown. This may take up to 40-45 minutes.

Drain off any oil which may appear, and spread the halva mixture onto a flat dish. Serve hot or cold, sprinkled with the pistachio nuts.

# SWEET SAFFRON RICE

*This is a sweet pilau, cooked using sugar instead of salt!*
*Wash the rice under running water until the water is clear.*

Serves 8-10

## INGREDIENTS

225g/8oz basmati rice
570ml/1 pint hot water
1 cinnamon stick, 2 inches long,
  broken into two pieces
4 whole cloves
¼ tsp saffron strands
45g/1½oz ghee or unsalted
  butter
1 tsp ground cardamom
¼ tsp ground nutmeg
120g/4oz caster sugar
60g/2oz raw cashews, split into
  halves
40g/1½oz seedless raisins or
  sultanas

Wash the rice and soak it in cold water for 30 minutes; drain thoroughly. Place the water, cinnamon, cloves and saffron in a saucepan and heat until boiling. Cover and leave to stand for 15 minutes.

Heat a large pan, add the ghee or butter and then add the rice. Fry for 3-4 minutes until it begins to look fairly dry. Stir frequently. Add the cardamom and nutmeg, stir and mix well. Add the sugar and the spiced liquid; then stir until the sugar is dissolved. Stir in the cashews and the raisins or sultanas. Cover and simmer gently for 10-12 minutes, then stand off the heat for a further 2-3 minutes. Fork through the rice, remove the cinnamon and cloves and serve.

# DURBARI MALPURA

*These are small pancakes covered in fruit, nuts and cream
and flavoured with nutmeg and orange rind.*

Serves 6

## INGREDIENTS

90g/3oz plain flour
30g/1oz ground rice
60g/2oz caster sugar
1 tsp ground or finely grated
  nutmeg
Pinch of bicarbonate of soda
Finely grated rind of 1 orange
30g/1oz raw cashews, lightly
  crushed
30g/1oz walnuts, lightly crushed
120ml/4 fl oz full-cream milk
Oil for deep-frying
15g/½oz butter
30g/1oz sultanas
30g/1oz flaked almonds
280ml/½ pint single cream
1 tbsp rose-water

Place the flour, ground rice,
sugar, nutmeg, bicarbonate of
soda, orange rind and the
crushed nuts in a bowl. Add the
milk and stir until a thick batter
is formed.

Heat the oil over a medium heat
in a deep frying pan. Add 1
heaped teaspoon of the batter at
a time until the whole pan is
filled with a single layer. When
the malpuras (spoonfuls of
batter) start floating to the
surface, turn them over. Fry
gently until golden brown on
both sides – about 5 minutes.
Drain on absorbent kitchen
paper.

Melt the butter over a low heat
and fry the sultanas for 1 minute.
Remove them with a slotted
spoon and drain on absorbent
kitchen paper. Fry the almonds
in the same fat until they are
lightly browned. Drain on
absorbent kitchen paper. Place
the cream in a saucepan large
enough to hold all the malpuras
and bring to a slow simmer. Add
the malpuras and stir gently.
Turn the entire contents of the
pan onto a warmed serving dish
and sprinkle the rose-water over
the top. Decorate with the fried
sultanas and the almonds. Serve
hot or cold.

# VERMICELLI KHEER

*Vermicelli are used in a number of popular Indian
puddings. This one is lightly spiced and creamy.*

Serves 6-8

### INGREDIENTS

2 tbsps ghee or unsalted butter
30g/1oz plain vermicelli
30g/1oz sultanas
30g/1oz almonds, blanched and
 slivered
570ml/1 pint full-cream milk
60g/2oz sugar
1 tbsp ground almonds
½ tsp ground cardamom seeds
½ tsp ground cinnamon
1 tbsp rose-water *or* 5-6 drops of
 vanilla or almond essence

Melt the ghee or butter in a pan
over a low heat and add the
vermicelli, sultanas and slivered
almonds. Stir fry until the
vermicelli are golden brown,
about 2-3 minutes. Add the milk,
sugar and ground almonds, bring
to the boil and simmer gently for
20 minutes, stirring frequently.
Stir in the ground cardamoms
and cinnamon and remove the
pan from heat. Allow the kheer
to cool slightly then stir in the
rose-water or other flavouring.
Serve hot or cold.

# FIRNI (CREAMED GROUND RICE WITH DRIED FRUIT AND NUTS)

*An aromatic rice pudding to serve hot or cold.*

Serves 6-8

*INGREDIENTS*
280ml/½ pint fresh milk
45g/1½oz ground rice
1 tbsp ground almonds
400g/14oz can evaporated milk
60g/2oz sugar
1 tbsp rose-water
1 tsp ground cardamom seeds
30g/1oz flaked almonds
30g/1oz pistachio nuts, lightly
   crushed
30g/1oz dried apricot, finely
   chopped

Place the milk in a heavy-based saucepan over a medium heat. Mix the ground rice and ground almonds together and sprinkle evenly over the milk, then bring it to the boil, stirring frequently. Add the evaporated milk and sugar, stir and cook over a low heat for 6-8 minutes. Remove the pan from the heat and allow the mixture to cool – stir occasionally to prevent a skin from forming. Stir in the rose-water and the ground cardamom, when cool.

Reserve a few almonds, pistachios and apricots and stir the remainder into the pudding. Transfer the firni to a serving dish and top with the reserved fruit and nuts. Serve hot or cold.

# SPICED MANGO FOOL

*Ripe mangoes eaten in their native country taste completely different! However, this spiced fool makes the most of canned fruits.*

Serves 6-8

## INGREDIENTS
2 tbsps milk
¼ tsp saffron strands
175g/6oz evaporated milk
60g/2oz sugar
1 tbsp fine semolina
2 tbsps ground almonds
1 tsp ground cardamom seeds
2 × 420g/15oz cans mangoes, drained and puréed
250g/9oz unflavoured fromage frais

Put the milk into a small saucepan and bring to the boil. Stir in the saffron strands, remove from the heat, cover the pan and set aside. Place the evaporated milk and sugar in a saucepan over a low heat. When it begins to bubble, sprinkle the semolina over the milk and stir until well blended, then add the ground almonds, stir and cook until the mixture thickens – this will take 5-6 minutes. Stir in the ground cardamoms and remove the pan from the heat. Allow to cool completely, then gradually beat in the mango purée, making sure there are no lumps.

In a large mixing bowl beat the fromage frais with a fork, then gradually beat in the evaporated milk and mango mixture. Stir in the saffron milk with all the strands as these will continue to impart their colour and flavour to the mango purée. Mix well. Spoon into a serving dish and chill for 2-3 hours.

# RASMALAI

*A classic Indian milk dessert, spiced with cardamoms which always cleanse the palate.*

Serves 4

*INGREDIENTS*
1.7 litres/3 pints milk
Lemon juice
2 tsps plain flour
8 green cardamoms, crushed
2-3 sugar cubes, cut in 12 small
  pieces

*Milk Sauce*
570ml/1 pint milk, reduced by
  boiling, to 430ml/¾ pint

*Syrup*
340g/12oz granulated sugar
280ml/½ pint water

*Decoration*
Few drops rosewater or orange
  flower water
30g/1oz pistachio nuts, chopped
30g/1oz almonds, chopped

Bring the 1.7 litres/3 pints of milk to the boil and add a little lemon juice. Leave to stand until separated. Cool for 10 minutes and then strain through a fine sieve or a clean piece of muslin. Leave to drain overnight.

Boil the milk for the sauce to reduce it and prepare the sugar syrup. Combine the granulated sugar and water in a saucepan and cook over a low heat for 2-3 minutes to dissolve the sugar. Bring to the boil and allow to boil for about 3 minutes or until syrupy.

Transfer the milk curds to a bowl and beat with an electric mixer or wooden spoon for about 5 minutes to soften. Add the flour and the cardamom seeds gradually, and continue beating. Leave for 2-3 minutes, then divide the mixture into 12. Place a piece of sugar cube in the centre of each portion, then press gently to flatten into 4cm/1½ inch rounds.

Bring the sugar syrup back to simmering point and drop in the rasmalai balls, a few at a time. Boil them for 10 minutes. Place the milk sauce in a serving dish. Remove the rasmalai from the syrup with a slotted spoon and place them in the milk sauce. When all the rasmalai are cooked and in the milk sauce, sprinkle with rose- or orange flower water and the chopped nuts. Allow to cool and refrigerate before serving.

# MELON BALLS IN MANGO PURÉE

*Melon and mango make a perfect partnership of flavours in this refreshing dessert.*

Serves 6

### INGREDIENTS
2 × 420g/15oz cans of sliced
 mangoes
1 galia or honeydew melon
Finely grated rind of 1 lemon
2 tbsps caster sugar
2 tbsps cornflour
½ tsp ground nutmeg
150ml/¼ pint double cream

Drain the canned mangoes and purée them in a liquidiser or food processor or push them through a sieve. Using a melon baller make as many balls as possible out of the melon. Scoop out any remaining flesh and blend in a liquidiser or food processor with any juice.

Transfer the melon purée to a saucepan and add the lemon rind and sugar. Blend the cornflour with a little water and add to the melon purée. Cook over low heat until the mixture thickens. Stir in the nutmeg and remove from the heat. Allow the mixture to cool slightly, then mix it with the mango purée.

Whip the cream until thick, then stir it into the mango mixture. Pour the melon and mango mixture into a flan dish and arrange the melon balls around the edge. Chill for 2-3 hours before serving.

# SHRIKAND

*This rich and creamy dessert is made from strained yogurt —
you will need a very fine muslin to strain the yogurt properly.*

Serves 6

### INGREDIENTS
3 × 420g/15oz cartons of thick-
　set natural yogurt
¼ tsp saffron strands
1 tbsp hot water
90g/3oz caster sugar
1 tbsp ground almonds
½ tsp ground cardamom seeds
¼ tsp grated or ground nutmeg

Pour the yogurt onto a clean,
very fine muslin cloth; bring
together the four corners of the
cloth so that the yogurt is held in
the middle. Tie the four corners
into a tight knot and hang the
muslin over the sink until all the
water content has been drained
off; this will take 4-6 hours or
can be done overnight.

Add the saffron strands to the hot
water, cover and set aside.
Carefully untie the muslin cloth
and empty the contents into a
mixing bowl. Beat the strained
yogurt with a fork, or a wire
beater, until smooth, then add
the sugar and mix thoroughly.
Add the ground almonds,
cardamom and the nutmeg and
mix well. Stir in the saffron
strands and the water in which it
was soaked. Chill before serving.

# SPICED FRUIT SALAD

*Most of the fruits required for this recipe are now available fresh, so use all fresh or a mixture of fresh and canned – whichever you prefer. Use apple juice if there is not syrup from the fruit.*

Serves 6-8

### INGREDIENTS

420g/15oz can pineapple chunks
420g/15oz can papaya (paw paw) chunks
420g/15oz can mango slices, cut into chunks
420g/15oz can guava halves, cut into chunks
3 cinnamon sticks, each 5cm/2 inches long
3 brown cardamoms
6 whole cloves
8 black peppercorns

Drain all the fruits and reserve the syrup. Mix all the syrups together and reserve 570ml/1 pint. Place the syrup in a saucepan and add the spices, bring to the boil, cover the pan and simmer for 20 minutes. Remove the lid of the pan and reduce the syrup to half of its original volume by boiling for 5-6 minutes. Remove from the heat and allow the syrup to cool. Cover the pan while the syrup cools – in an open pan some of the flavour would be lost. Reserve a few pieces of papaya and guava and all the mango. Arrange the remaining fruits in a serving bowl. Arrange the mangoes on top, then add the reserved papaya and guava. Strain the spiced syrup over the fruits. Cover and chill before serving.

# MANGO DELIGHT

*I prefer to use fresh mangoes for this dessert, but only if they are really ripe. If not, use canned mangoes but you may need slightly to reduce the sugar in the recipe to compensate for the sweetness of the syrup.*

Serves 4-6

### INGREDIENTS

2 fresh ripe mangoes *or* 2 42g/15oz cans of sliced mangoes
2 tbsps custard powder
2 tbsps sugar
150ml/¼ pint milk
1 tsp ground cardamoms or mixed spice
150ml/¼ pint double cream
2 tbsps shelled unsalted pistachio nuts, lightly crushed

Drain one can of the mango slices and purée them in a liquidiser or food processor. Drain the other can and coarsely chop the mango slices. If using fresh mangoes, peel and slice them. Mix the custard powder and sugar together, then gradually add the milk and blend well. Cook over a low heat until the consistency resembles whipped cream, then stir in the ground cardamoms or mixed spice and remove from the heat. Gradually add the mango pulp, or the chopped flesh of one of the mangoes to the custard mix, stirring all the time.

Whisk the cream until fairly thick, but still of a pouring consistency. If you buy extra thick double cream, there is no need to whisk it. Stir the cream into the mango mixture and gently mix in the remaining chopped mangoes. Transfer the mango mixture to a serving bowl and top with the crushed pistachio nuts. Serve hot or cold.

# SEMOLINA AND ALMOND HALVA

*Halva is very rich and very sweet – serve only small pieces and keep any remaining halva well chilled.*

Serves 6-8

### INGREDIENTS
120g/4oz ghee or unsalted butter
120g/4oz fine semolina
120g/4oz ground almonds
120g/4oz sugar
½ tsp ground nutmeg
280ml/10 fl oz full-cream milk
30g/1oz raw cashews, chopped

Grease a large plate and set it to one side. Melt the ghee or butter in a saucepan over a low heat. Add the semolina and cook for 6-7 minutes, stirring continuously until golden brown. Add the almonds, sugar and nutmeg, stir and mix thoroughly, then add the milk and mix, stirring until the mixture thickens and stops sticking to the bottom and sides of the pan.

Put the mixture onto the greased plate and spread it evenly to about 1.25cm/½ inch thickness; use the back of a lightly greased metal spoon to do this. Using a knife, press the sides inwards to form a large square. Sprinkle the chopped cashews evenly over the halva and press them in gently with the palm of your hand. Allow the mixture to cool and cut into 2.5cm/1 inch squares.

# SWEET VERMICELLI

*This dish is a Muslim speciality and is always made during the festival of 'Idd Ul Fitr'.*

Serves 6

### INGREDIENTS

120g/4oz plain vermicelli
60g/2oz ghee or unsalted butter
30g/1oz sultanas
30g/1oz raw cashew nuts, split or coarsely chopped
30g/1oz blanched almonds, split whole or coarsely chopped or flaked almonds
4 green cardamom pods, split open at the top
½ tsp ground cardamom seeds
½ tsp ground nutmeg
280ml/½ pint water
60g/2oz sugar

Break the vermicelli into small pieces. Melt 15g/½oz ghee or butter over low heat and fry the sultanas until they swell up. Remove the pan from heat and transfer the sultanas to a plate with a slotted spoon. Place the pan back over the heat, add all the nuts and stir fry until the nuts turn slightly brown. Transfer them with a slotted spoon to another dish. Return the pan to the heat again and add the remaining ghee or butter. Increase the heat to medium, add the whole cardamom and fry for 30 seconds. Add the vermicelli and fry until a rich golden colour, stirring constantly – this will take about 5 minutes.

Remove the pan from the heat, add the sultanas, half the fried nuts, ground cardamom and the ground nutmeg and stir briskly. Return the pan to the heat and add the water and sugar. Bring to the boil, cover the pan and simmer for 5 minutes. Remove the lid, adjust the heat to medium and cook the vermicelli for 2-3 minutes or until the liquid dries up, stirring constantly. Serve hot or cold. If serving cold, use a fork to separate the vermicelli strands as they will stick together when cold. Decorate with the remaining fried nuts.

# COCONUT STUFFED PANCAKES

*These lightly spiced pancakes are rather different to the ones you might serve on Shrove Tuesday, but they are bound to be popular with all the family at any time of the year.*

Makes 6 pancakes

### INGREDIENTS
#### For the Filling
60g/2oz desiccated coconut
60g/2oz soft dark brown sugar
30g/1oz walnut pieces, lightly
  crushed
170g/6oz can evaporated milk
1 tsp ground cardamom seeds

Mix all the ingredients, except the ground cardamom, in a small saucepan and place over medium heat. As soon as the mixture begins to bubble, reduce the heat and let it simmer without a lid for 8-10 minutes, stirring occasionally. Stir in the ground cardamoms, remove the pan from the heat and allow the mixture to cool.

#### For the Pancakes
2 eggs
175g/6oz wholemeal flour
1 tsp ground cinnamon
1 tbsp caster sugar
200ml/7 fl oz milk
Ghee or unsalted butter for
  frying

Place all ingredients, except the ghee or butter, in a large bowl and beat with a wire whisk until smooth. This batter can also be prepared in a liquidiser or food processor. Place a non-stick or cast iron frying pan over a low heat and, when hot, melt a little ghee or butter on it, about ¼ of a teaspoon. Pour 2 tablespoons of the batter into the pan and spread it quickly by tilting the pan, to prevent it from setting before you have a chance to spread it. The pancake will set in a minute or so, let it cook for a further minute, then carefully turn it over with a thin spatula, or toss it! Cook the other side for about 1 minute (brown spots should appear on both sides). Spread 1 tablespoon of the filling on one side of the pancake and roll it up. Make the rest of the pancakes in the same way.

# KULFI
# (INDIAN ICE CREAM)

*This is the most popular ice cream in India! It is firmer than most ice creams and needs to be kept in the refrigerator for around 90 minutes before serving.*

Serves 6-8

### INGREDIENTS
150ml/¼ pint fresh milk
2 tbsps ground rice
1 tbsp ground almonds
410g/14oz can evaporated milk
1 tsp ground cardamom seeds
60g/2oz sugar
430ml/¾ pint double cream
1 tbsp rose-water or 5-6 drops of
   any other flavouring such as
   vanilla, almond etc.
30g/1oz shelled, unsalted
   pistachio nuts, lightly crushed

Heat the milk until it is lukewarm. Place the ground rice and ground almonds in a small bowl and gradually add the warm milk, a little at a time, to make a thin paste of pouring consistency. Stir continuously to break up any lumps. If any lumps remain, sieve the mixture.

Heat the evaporated milk to boiling point and add the ground cardamom. Take the pan off the heat and gradually add the almond and rice mixture, stirring continuously. Add the sugar and cream and place the pan over a medium heat to cook the mixture for 12-15 minutes, stirring continuously. Remove the pan from heat and allow the mixture to cool slightly. Add the rose-water or other flavouring and half of the pistachio nuts, stir and mix well. Allow the mixture to cool completely, stirring frequently to prevent a skin from forming on the surface.

When the mixture has cooled completely, put it into a plastic ice cream box or individual moulds. Top with the remaining pistachio nuts and place in the freezer for 4-5 hours. Place the kulfi in the refrigerator for 1½ hours before serving. This will soften it slightly and make it easier to cut. The time required to soften the kulfi will vary according to the size of the container used for freezing.

# STUFFED LYCHEES

*Lychees grow throughout India and are a popular dessert –
just the ripe fruit enjoyed on its own. It is easier to use
canned lychees if you want to stuff the fruits – they are
pitted before canning and are therefore much easier
to prepare.*

Serves 4-6

### INGREDIENTS
2×430g/15oz cans lychees
1 fresh mango *or* 430g/15oz can
   sliced mangoes
2 tbsps cornflour
Finely grated rind of 1 lemon
2 tbsps lemon juice
150ml/¼ pint double cream
A few drops of yellow food
   colouring (optional)
1 tbsp ground almonds
Toasted flaked almonds to
   decorate (optional)

Drain the lychees and the
mangoes and reserve 175ml/6 fl
oz lychee and 120ml/4 fl oz
mango syrup. Mix the syrups
together and keep to one side. If
using fresh mango, reserve all
the juice from the lychees and
make up to 280ml/½ pint by
adding cold water. Place the
cornflour in a saucepan and add
a little syrup to make a smooth
paste. Gradually add the rest of
the syrup and mix thoroughly.
Add the lemon rind and juice
and cook over low heat until the
mixture boils and thickens. Allow
to cool.

Beat the cream until thick, then
stir it into the cornflour mixture
with the food colouring. Add the
ground almonds and mix well.
Remove any broken lychees,
chop them finely and add them
to the cornflour mixture. Reserve
the whole lychees. Chop the
mango slices roughly.

Stuff each whole lychee with
chopped mangoes so that the
mango stands about 6mm/¼ inch
proud of each lychee. Add any
remaining mango pieces or pulp
to the cornflour mixture. Line a
25cm/10 inch flan dish with the
cornflour mixture and arrange
the lychees on top (the cornflour
mixture will line a smaller dish
rather too thickly and the lychees
will sink). Chill before serving.

# WHEAT FUDGE

*Use a very fine wholemeal flour for this recipe – a bread flour simply will not work as it contains too much coarse bran. Chapati flour is ideal.*

Serves 10-12

## INGREDIENTS

120g/4oz ghee or unsalted butter
225g/8oz fine textured
    wholemeal flour
1½ tsps ground cardamom seeds
30g/1oz chopped mixed nuts
120g/4oz light brown sugar

Melt the ghee in a saucepan over a medium heat and add the flour, stir and mix thoroughly. Cook for 5 minutes, stirring continuously. Reduce the heat to low and cook for a further 10-12 minutes, stirring continuously. Add the cardamom and chopped nuts, stir and cook for 2-3 minutes, then remove from the heat and add the sugar. Mix well, and if there are any lumps, break them up with the back of the spoon.

Lightly grease a large plate and spread the flour mixture on it. Using the back of a metal spoon, spread the mixture evenly to form a large square, about 1.25cm/½ inch thick, 15cm/6 inches wide and 20cm/8 inches long. Allow the mixture to cool, then chill for 20 minutes. Remove from the refrigerator and cut into 4-5cm/1½-2 inch squares. Allow to harden before serving. Store in an open container or plate in the refrigerator. The fudge will keep for 3-4 weeks.

# JEERA PANI

*Cumin has always been noted for its ability to aid digestion
– this is cumin water, a good appetizer to serve before a
heavy meal.*

Serves 4

*INGREDIENTS*
2 tbsps cumin seeds
570ml/1 pint water
2-3 dried red chillies
15g/½oz freshly chopped mint
   leaves, *or* 1 tsp dried mint
1 tsp salt
1 tsp sugar
1 tbsp lemon juice

Heat a cast iron, or heavy-based pan and dry-roast the cumin seeds until they are a shade darker. Crush them lightly in a pestle and mortar. Bring the water to the boil in a saucepan, add the cumin, chillies, mint, salt and sugar, then cover the pan and simmer for 15 minutes. Stir in the lemon juice then remove the pan from the heat. Allow the drink to cool, then strain it into individual glasses.

# SPICY PINEAPPLE PUNCH

*Pineapples are the traditional symbol of hospitality – this is
an excellent drink with which to greet your friends.*

Serves 6-8

### INGREDIENTS
430ml/¾ pint water
1 litre/1¾ pints pineapple juice
5 cinnamon sticks, 5cm/2 inches
   long; broken up
12 whole cloves
12 green cardamoms, bruised
15g/½oz freshly chopped mint
   leaves
175ml/6fl oz brandy

Place the water, half the
pineapple juice, cinnamon,
cloves, cardamom and mint in a
saucepan. Bring to the boil,
cover the pan and simmer gently
for 20 minutes. Remove from the
heat and allow to cool, keeping
the pan covered. Strain the drink
and add the remaining pineapple
juice and the brandy. Mix well
and chill before serving.

# NIMBU PANI

*This is an Indian lemonade, a spicy refreshing drink for hot weather.*

Serves 4

*INGREDIENTS*
2 tbsps caster sugar
1 tsp salt
570ml/1 pint water
Juice of 1 lemon
Crushed ice
4 slices of lemon

Place the sugar and salt in the water and stir until dissolved, then stir in the lemon juice. Place the crushed ice in individual glasses and strain the nimbu pani into the glasses over the ice. Top with the sliced lemon and serve.

# MANGO SHERBET

*This recipe makes a thick sherbert drink with the luxurious flavour of mango. Thin it down with more milk if preferred, or top with a scoop of vanilla ice cream.*

Serves 4-6

*INGREDIENTS*
2×420g/15oz cans of sliced
  mangoes, drained
570ml/1 pint milk
4 tbsps caster sugar
1 tsp ground cardamom seeds
1 tbsp rose-water (optional)
280ml/½ pint cold water

Place the mango slices, half the milk, sugar, cardamom and rose-water in a liquidiser or food processor and blend for a few seconds. Transfer the contents to a large jug or bowl and add the remaining milk and water. Chill for 2-3 hours before serving.

# RASAM

*This is a hot drink flavoured with lentils and seasoned with spiced oil.*

Serves 4-6

*INGREDIENTS*
850ml/1½ pints water
60g/2oz masoor dhal (red split
  lentils), washed and drained
1 tsp coriander seeds
1 tsp cumin seeds
2 dried red chillies
6-8 curry leaves
1 level tsp tamarind concentrate
  *or* 1 tbsp lemon juice
1 tsp salt
1 tsp paprika
1 tbsp cooking oil
½ tsp black mustard seeds

Place the water, dhal, coriander, cumin, chillies and curry leaves in a saucepan and bring to the boil.

Reduce the heat to medium and cook, uncovered, for 6-8 minutes. Cover the pan and simmer for 30 minutes. Remove the pan from the heat and allow to cool slightly. Strain the liquid and sieve the dhal into it. Return it to the pan, heat and add the tamarind or lemon juice, salt and paprika. Stir until the tamarind is dissolved.

Heat the oil in a separate pan and add the mustard seeds. As soon as the seeds crackle, add the rasam or stir the hot oil and the seeds into the rasam. Remove from heat and serve warm.

# SPICED TEA

*Spiced or flavoured teas have long been popular drinks in India – I use Assam tea in this recipe.*

Serves 2

### INGREDIENTS
430ml/¾ pint water
6 whole cloves
6 green cardamoms, bruised
1 cinnamon stick, 5cm/2-inches long, broken up
3 tsps tea leaves or 2 tea bags
Milk and sugar to taste

Place the water in a saucepan and bring to the boil. Add the spices, cover the pan and simmer for 10 minutes. Rinse a teapot with hot water and add the tea leaves or the tea bags. Bring the spiced liquid to the boil again and strain it into the teapot. Brew for 5 minutes and serve with milk and sugar to taste.

# INDEX